worth
  writing
about

worth writing about

exploring memoir with adolescents

jake wizner

STENHOUSE PUBLISHERS
PORTLAND, MAINE

Stenhouse Publishers
www.stenhouse.com

Library of Congress Cataloging-in-Publication Data
Wizner, Jake.
  Worth writing about : exploring memoir with adolescents / Jake Wizner.
     pages cm
  Includes bibliographical references and index.
  ISBN 978-1-62531-048-4 (pbk. : alk. paper) -- ISBN 978-1-62531-049-1 (ebook) 1. English language--Composition and exercises--Study and teaching (Secondary) 2. Biography as a literary form--Study and teaching (Secondary)--United States. 3. Language arts (Secondary)--Curricula--United States. I. Title.
   LB1631.W569 2015
   808'.0420712--dc23

2015003862

Cover and interior design by Blue Design (www.bluedes.com)

Manufactured in the United States of America

PRINTED ON 30% PCW
RECYCLED PAPER

21 20 19 18 17 16 15   9 8 7 6 5 4 3 2 1

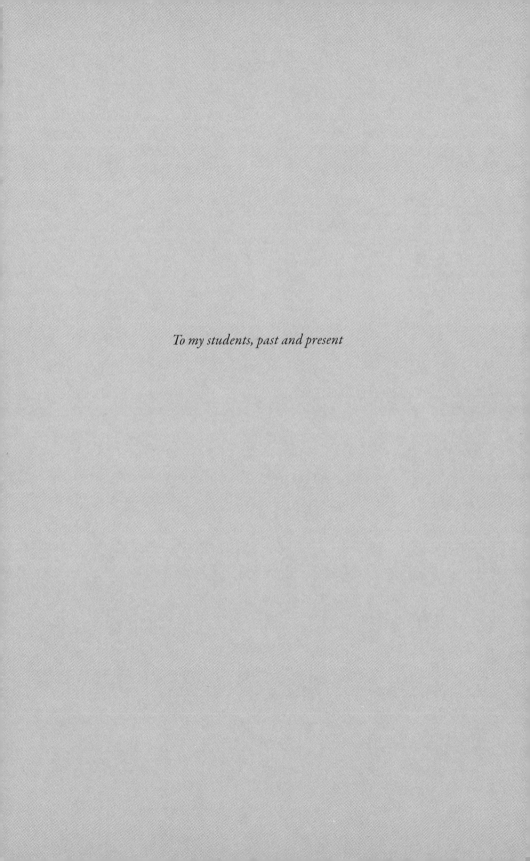

To my students, past and present

CONTENTS

Acknowledgments

When I decided to show this book to publishers, my assistant principal, Jennifer Goodwin, suggested I send it to Maureen Barbieri at Stenhouse.

"You probably know Maureen," she said.

"I've actually never met her," I admitted. "But I know the name."

"Oh, I think you'll really like her," Jennifer said. "She's wonderful."

My wife, a former teacher, was even more emphatic. "You don't know Maureen? How is that possible? She worked with us in District 2. I love her."

It took me about two e-mail exchanges with Maureen to join the circle of fans and admirers. Thank you, Maureen, for taking me under your wing and guiding me through the publication of this book with unflagging patience, wisdom, and warmth. I am lucky to have you as an editor, and even luckier to count you as a friend.

Through Maureen, I've gradually become acquainted with the team at Stenhouse. Special thanks to Dan Tobin, who championed this book from the beginning, and to Chris Downey, Jay Kilburn, Louisa Irele, Jill Cooley, and Rebecca Eaton for all they have done to help usher this book into the world.

I have been fortunate to spend the past nineteen years teaching at the wonderful Salk School of Science in downtown Manhattan. Thank you to Salk's visionary founding principal, Alexis Penzell, who hired me when the school was brand new and encouraged me to teach memoir writing to the very first eighth-grade class. Thank you to Salk's current principal, Rhonda Perry, who has done so much over the past fourteen years to shape Salk into the loving, intellectually vigorous, and fun place it is today. And thank you to all of my amazing colleagues at Salk, who make coming to work each day a joy. It's a privilege to spend my days alongside people I like and respect so much.

I've dedicated this book to my students, and I want to acknowledge, in particular, the many students whose work I have included. Thank you for giving me permission to share your stories. Your words, as much as mine, are the reason this book exists.

My parents were my first and toughest editors as I was growing up, so it was immensely encouraging when they read an early draft of the book and gushed about how much they loved it. Thank you, Mom and Dad, for all of your love and support, and for always making me feel that teaching is such a noble profession.

And, of course, thank you, Kira, Leilani, and Cecily. You fill my life with moments worth writing about.

The Rice Bowl

It is the first day of our memoir unit, and I stand in front of my eighth-grade class holding the memoir of a student I taught seventeen years ago. I'm feeling the excitement I always feel when I launch this unit. Even though each year's classes are different, even though I know I can't anticipate everything that will happen as students grapple with putting their lives on paper, I know from experience that the next two months will be the most memorable, most meaningful, and most exciting work we do all year.

"I want to start today by reading a memoir that one of my past students wrote when she was in my eighth-grade class," I tell my students. "This is the end product. This is where you'll be in about two months."

I show them the title page. It has the memoir's title, *The Rice Bowl,* next to a picture of a winged creature. A caption reads: *The phoenix, a mythological female bird reborn from fire and ashes.* The bottom third of the page contains a family photograph of the writer, her three sisters, and her mother standing together and smiling.

On the next page there is a dedication to her mother and her sisters, and to the New York Asian Women's Center "as a thank you for all that you have done for us." My students are attentive, curious to hear what a past student wrote and to understand what this memoir unit is all about.

"She begins her memoir with a fifteen-sentence portrait," I say. "Remember the ones we did earlier this year in writing workshop?"

They nod, eager for me to get on with it.

I turn the page and begin to read . . .

"GRAY"

You stand there in the shadow of my mind.

Your dark brown eyes look upon me every time I think of you.

I can only imagine you with clutched fist.

You are like a hunter, and I'm the prey.

I remember when you used to hold me as a child, watching me wherever I would go and never paying attention to anyone or anything else.

I never believed this would happen.

I still remember the smell of your shirt and the yellowish green of the sweat.

I wish to see you in your grave; that would be paying for all you have done.

You are the top of the food chain, like a lion eating away at me.

You are a snake, slithering in the grass, waiting to strike at my weakness and leaving me to suffer.

You went away, leaving us to survive on our own, to die.

After you had gone the sweet smell of flowers came back, the colors brightly shone.

We are the colorful flowers, and you are the wilting petals.

I never want to see you again – only when you finally rest in peace.

The grayness of your heart shows who you really are.

The Rice Bowl

At first I didn't really know what was going on. It wasn't until I lost my father that everything else went with him — my sisters, my mom, everything. My life started to fall apart.

❊   ❊

Growing up in a household being the youngest was quite good, except for the fact that I wasn't old enough for anything. I always had my oldest sister, Anna, to watch me, as if I were her own. Jessica was always helping out Anna, and most of the time she was there to monitor me. Wendy was the one who would get jealous once in a while for attention, but she was always there to play with me. My mother, to me, was always the one running things and making sure everything was okay. My father, well, he was just there, never paying much attention to me or anyone else beside himself.

✳   ✳   ✳

It all started over rice. Nights of waking up sweating and crying, nights of nightmares replaying in my mind. I was five years old when it happened. I don't remember much, but for many years that night replayed in my head over and over again. To think, a five-year-old, watching her horrors begin and not knowing they would follow her for the rest of her life.

I came home one night to the basement of my uncle's house from school. Even though we were my uncle's family, my spineless father was too afraid to stand up to his own brother, so we were stuck living in his cramped basement. (I can still smell the scent of wet cement and sand from the unfinished walls.) We were all home that night – my father, my mother, my three sisters, and me.

It all started over rice.

That night my father demanded that my mother cook rice and make dinner. She was so tired of following his demands and just tired in general so she refused. My oldest sister, Anna, jumped in to help cook. She was speaking to my father in the kitchen while making dinner. My mom and Jessica were in the other room. Wendy and I were playing, but she had moved to the kitchen when it happened. I was near the staircase listening, my nightmares about to begin. Anna told my father that we shouldn't cook because every night as we were eating, our brat cousin would jump up and down on our ceiling to make the sand fall on our table. She asked him why he wouldn't say anything and why he was afraid to stand up to his brother. Since my father was a short-tempered man he became furious. He had been raised to think that no woman could stand up to a man, and since my sister was telling him what to do, this obviously struck his ego. Not only was he an egotistical man, he was also an abusive one. He slapped my sister in the face for what she said. She was scared so she ran in the room screaming for my mother. I didn't see what was going on in the room, but I heard screaming and bangs on the wall.

My mother later told me that my father kept hitting my sister and banging her head against the wall. She told me that usually when he would hit her she would be scared, but this time he was hitting my sister. Like any person would do, my mother tried to stop him. She wrestled with him for a while and managed to push him out of the room. I peered out and saw him walking to the kitchen. I tried to cover my ears to block off the cries that shook my body. The next thing I knew there was a sharp scream from my sister Wendy who was in the kitchen, and then I saw my father walking toward the room with a meat cleaver in his hand.

Before he walked in the room I knew my mother was alert that something was wrong from the scream. He tried to kill Anna, threatening her with the knife. My mother came out of nowhere and grabbed his hand with the knife in it, then grabbed him by the throat. She grabbed him away from Anna and pushed him against the wall on the side of the stairs. I was beside the room and right in front by the stairs. I saw as my mom struggled with him and then threatened to kill him if anything were to happen to any of us. After she threatened him, she forced him to drop the knife. (Every now and then I can still hear the metal hitting the ground.) She pulled him up the stairs and pushed him out the door. He tried to push his way back in but my mom would not let him. He broke a hole in the door and ran down the stairs. Looking as if he was about to explode, he started yelling and screaming again, but this time my mom yelled back. She told him to get out once and for all, looking like a mad woman. From the look on his face, I could tell he was afraid. She escorted him out roughly and told him not to come back until he cooled down.

I waited for a while to see if it was safe. Then I ran into the room crying and saw everyone else crying too. That night I cried myself to sleep with my sisters beside me, but it wasn't over. While sleeping, the image of my father coming toward the room with a knife kept replaying. What happened to the caring father that I thought loved us? Even to this day I still wonder how a person who gave you life would be willing to take it back in a flash. For a while it was quiet, but the racket and roaring of my dreams awoke me.

Anna was so afraid she tried to leave. She called her gang over to pick her up, but my mother wouldn't let her go. She wouldn't let this take her daughter away forever. My father came home about three-in-the-morning with his family beside him. Anna was still in shock so she stayed in the room. My mother went to see what he and his family wanted. Everyone thought my mother was crazy that night, especially my father, because this was the first time she had ever fought back. His sister tried to get in the room, but my mother pushed her away. Then as everyone tried to take Wendy and me away, my mother sprung into action. She hollered at them and tried to hold them back. As she couldn't hold against them any longer, she yelled to my sister Jessica, telling her that if anyone tried to get past the door to kill them.

After everyone heard that, they knew my mother was hysterical. Eventually they all left, including my father. She saw them out the door, but as my father stepped out, he turned around and asked my mom for the medical cards. My mom guessed he planned this out with his family, because he knew that Anna needed to see the doctor, badly.

✻   ✻   ✻   ✻

That was the last time I saw my father. The lasting image I have of him is with a knife in his hand. I always had the chance to see him, but I never dared. What would happen if I did? That is a question I always had in mind. Would he have kidnapped me? Would he have loved me? Or would he have killed me? I try to imagine what it would be like actually to see him, but I'm afraid that if I wanted to see him, my mother would go ballistic.

✻   ✻   ✻   ✻   ✻

We ran away from my father but we had no place to go. Since we had just moved to the United States, my mom didn't speak a word of English. She had very little education and no job or money. Luckily, my mom got in touch with a foundation called the New York Asian Women's Center, a type of women's shelter. That was the only alternative we had. After we left, my mother started to go into depression. Hours of her just staring into space crying made me want to cry. Watching her feel sad and not being able to help made me feel helpless and pitiful. So what was I to do? For a long time, I tried to forget it and push it aside, but it didn't help. Everything around reminded me of the situation. After accepting the fact that I was fatherless, I now had to accept the fact that we were also homeless.

Eventually things became worse. My two older sisters ran away from home for many months. For a while it was just the three of us. Three bowls, three plates, and three cups. I still remember the three bowls my mom bought with blue rimming. Every time I saw those bowls I couldn't help but to think about my sisters. Almost *every night my mom called the police reporting my sisters missing, but they were nowhere to be found. Those months were so horrible. My mom acted as if nothing was wrong, but I saw in her eyes that a part of her was missing.*

I don't remember what happened, but all I know and really cared about was that they finally came back. After they came back, we finally moved out of the shelter and into our own apartment. Once we settled into our new apartment, things started to change again. My second oldest sister, Jessica, became very quiet and hardly spoke a word. My oldest sister, Anna, became rebellious and started many fights with my mother and Jessica. The fights got so out of hand that many times our neighbors would call the police. All night shouting and crying would make everyone crazy, especially my mom. One time I got so sick of crying and hearing them argue, I made myself throw up. That got them to stop, but they went berserk to see what was wrong with me.

For about two years the fighting occurred and for two years my mom tried to get all of us to family therapy. Every time any type of arguing or fighting would occur, my mom would blame it on my father and say my sister Anna was crazy. I always knew that wasn't true. The fighting did occur because of my father, but I never believed her when she called my sister crazy. I loved Anna even though she did so many things that I didn't understand. At that time I never understood how any of the fights started, but now I realize why they happened. All my mom wanted was to watch us grow up in a good and safe environment. She worked so hard to lead us somewhere better, she didn't want to give up. After she realized she had lost my father, she pushed even harder. I guess that was what drove Anna and Jessica away.

    ✻   ✻   ✻   ✻   ✻   ✻

Recently things have started to run smoothly. Now that everyone except me is almost old enough to live on her own, there is less friction between all of us. My mom can now accept the fact that she can't push too hard to see what she wants and can't always impose on us her expectations. Anna is now working and partially supporting the family and playing a motherly role in my life. Jessica is in college working for her degree and Wendy is about to start college, and just about to take charge in her life as an adult.

I can now accept the fact that all of us lost a father, not just me, and I'm not alone to face my fears. Hatred, forgiveness, and pity are all feelings I have toward him. Now that he has a new wife and children again, I can only feel sorrow for his new wife, who doesn't know what kind of man he really is.

Though our family has separated numerous times, there are still borders that none of us can pass to get away. Like rice in a rice bowl, it is always held together as a whole.

I look up and experience that magical moment of a room full of students, transfixed, transported, and—perhaps—transformed by what they have just heard. It is the first of many magical moments that will happen in my classroom over the next two months.

The memoir unit has begun.

CHAPTER 1

Why Memoir?

When I began teaching eighth-grade English at the Salk School of Science in Manhattan in 1996, the school had been open for just one year. It had expanded from sixty students in grades six and seven in year one to 180 students in grades six, seven, and eight in year two. Of the original three teachers, two had left, and a new staff of eight was in a position to shape what the school should look like and determine what should be taught. Because the school had been established in partnership with the NYU Medical School, more thought had been put into the science curriculum than into anything else. Our principal and the staff at NYU had conceived the idea that all graduating eighth graders should put together a science exit piece—some kind of project that they could present to a panel of experts and answer questions about. Would it be possible, my principal asked me, to do something similar in English Language Arts? She had an idea that perhaps it could be some kind of memoir writing, since eighth grade marked the end of one phase of our students' lives and would give them an opportunity to look back and reflect on their experiences to date.

I was skeptical. Eighth grade, it seemed to me, was far too young an age to write memoir. Was it possible that thirteen-year-old children had had enough meaningful experiences and the necessary distance from those experiences to be able to write reflectively about them? What would I have written about at that age? My life at that point had been relatively uneventful, and anything that might have made a compelling story revolved around insecurities that I was still harboring and would never have been willing to share. Still, at my principal's urging, I agreed to do a six-week study of memoir in May and June that would revolve around students writing their own memoirs and presenting them in some sort of public forum. If the unit turned out to be unsuccessful, then I would come up with another final English project for the following year that would be more age appropriate.

That was 1996. Fast forward to spring, 2014. I stand in front of my eighth graders and tell them that this is my favorite time of the year. I tell them that for the next eight to ten weeks (yes, the unit has grown longer) we will be immersing ourselves in memoir—reading it, writing it, thinking about it, discussing it. I tell them that at the end of the unit most of them will have produced the best piece of writing they have ever produced, and many of them will have come to see themselves and their lives in new ways. They look at me skeptically. How do I know this will happen? I know it, I say, because it happens every year.

Memoir Writing and the Common Core

I had been teaching memoir writing for many, many years before the Common Core State Standards (NGA/CCSSO 2012a) swept across the nation's educational landscape with tornado force. Since that time, schools across the country have been revamping curriculum, retraining teachers, and retooling tests to meet the demands of these new, more rigorous learning standards. I have been part of this revolution, working with colleagues and administrators and staff developers to deepen my understanding of the Common Core and to use the standards to sharpen and refine many of the units I teach.

Memoir writing fits well with the Common Core. The third writing standard (listed as *CCSS.ELA-Literacy W.8.3* for the eighth grade) deals with narrative writing, and all of the specific narrative writing skills that the Common Core lays out (listed in the standards as *W.8.3.A, W.8.3.B, W.8.3.C, W.8.3.D,* and *W.8.3.E*) can easily be targeted in a memoir writing unit. In fact, Appendix A to the standards (NGA/CCSSO 2010b) explicitly states: "In English language arts, students produce narratives that take the form of creative fictional stories, memoirs, anecdotes, and autobiographies."

There are more general writing standards that can also be targeted. Writing standards 4 and 5 (*CCSS.ELA-Literacy.W.8.4* and *CCSS.ELA-Literacy.W.8.5*), which describe skills related to the production and distribution of writing, align neatly with the memoir writing process. So as I looked at the work I was doing, it was a relief to see that in many ways it was already compatible with the Common Core.

But whatever gratification I felt soon began to dissipate as I started using the standards to rethink my main objectives in teaching the unit. It wasn't that I disliked the standards or couldn't figure out how to make them fit the unit I had developed. It was more a feeling that the value of memoir writing transcended the list of writing skills the Common Core laid out. Memoir was more than just one of many genres that could be used to target narrative writing standards. It was more than just a cursory mention in Appendix A. It was more than just one possible means to an end. Memoir writing was an end in itself. Whether or not it aligned perfectly with the Common Core was of secondary importance.

I understand that not everybody will accept this argument. The Common Core has become a form of gospel in many education circles, and its strongest proponents would consider sacrilegious the suggestion that writing as a vehicle for self-exploration and self-discovery has as much educational value as developing the specific skills deemed necessary for success in college and beyond. My belief is that the Common Core standards are an extremely important addition to an ongoing conversation about teaching and learning, but they should not eclipse all other ideas about the purposes of education and the many objectives we have as teachers. As Kelly Gallagher wryly observes in *Write Like This*, few of us would really want to encounter a former student twenty years after teaching her and have her say, "Oh, it is so good to see you! I was hoping to run into you someday so that I can tell you that I am still writing essays that analyze the author's use of tone" (2011, 9). How much more satisfying to run into that same student and have her say, "Oh, it's so good to see you! I was hoping to run into you someday so that I can tell you that you were the teacher who made me love writing for the first time and showed me that writing could be so much more than just something I had to do for school."

So while this book does, indirectly, speak to several of the writing standards in the Common Core (and even more indirectly to several of the reading standards), the focus lies elsewhere. For as much as memoir writing can be a vehicle through which to teach specific skills, there are reasons to teach memoir writing that are even more important.

Five Reasons I Teach Memoir Writing

1. MEMOIR WRITING HELPS STUDENTS ANSWER THE QUESTION, "WHO AM I?"

Throughout middle school, students are constantly inventing and reinventing themselves. They are developing physically and hormonally, becoming more conscious of how they appear to others, gaining new freedoms and responsibilities, and struggling to balance the increasing demands being placed on them both socially and academically. Who they are in the classroom is not the same as who they are in the hallways, or at the dinner table, or on Facebook, or in bed at night. They are full of insecurities even as they project cockiness, crave the spotlight while doing everything they can to blend in, and cry out against prejudice and injustice while calling each other gay and promoting things like "hug a Jew day."

Eighth grade is a real transition point for my students; the turbulent years of middle school are coming to a close, and high school is looming just ahead. And as their lives continue to rush by, it becomes hugely important for young teenagers to have the space and opportunity to look back, take stock, and think deeply about the choices they have made, the identities they have tried on, and the young adults they are becoming.

In *The Art of Teaching Writing*, Lucy Calkins observes: "I think that during adolescence we have a special need to understand our lives, to find a plot line in the complexity of events, to see coordinates of continuity amid the discontinuity. During adolescence, youngsters construct a sense of personal identity. It is a time for trying on selves, for reflection, self-awareness, and self-definition. The adolescent learns to say, 'This is my story' and 'This is who I am'" (1994, 158). Memoir writing allows this to happen.

2. MEMOIR WRITING BUILDS COMMUNITY IN THE CLASSROOM

During the year, we read excerpts from Melba Pattillo Beals's memoir, *Warriors Don't Cry* (1994). She describes the unrelenting prejudice she experiences as one of nine black students integrating an all-white high school. My students

< 11 >

talk about how so much of the hatred and distrust stems from ignorance. If these white students had grown up going to school with black students, they might realize that they have more in common than they think. The more we know each other, the more we are able to recognize the common humanity that binds us all together.

Eighth graders fall easily into cliques, find security in their small groups of friends. They know the names of their other classmates, know what they look like and what kinds of students they are, but know very little of their internal lives. When students write their memoirs, they are revealing themselves in new and profound ways to their classmates. A girl who is often disrespectful to her teachers and seems to care much more about her social life than her academic one confesses that she wishes she could go back to being the good girl she was when she was younger. A boy who rarely speaks in class writes about how he practices having conversations with himself in the mirror to improve his social skills. A seemingly independent girl who goes through each day with a smile on her face describes how socially isolated she feels, and a boy who projects stoicism breaks down and cries as he reads about the death of his grandfather. In each of these cases, students begin to look at each other with newfound respect or understanding or sympathy or appreciation. New bonds form. Students recognize that many of their own fears and insecurities are common among their classmates. They learn that some of their peers have parents that are divorced or family relationships that are strained. Like a platoon of soldiers that goes through a battle together and becomes more strongly bonded by the shared experience, so too do stronger bonds grow among a group of teenagers who write and share their memoirs, revealing themselves to each other in deeply personal ways.

3. MEMOIR WRITING IS A GENRE THAT IS HIGHLY ACCESSIBLE TO ALL STUDENTS

While middle school students might be naturally drawn to writing fiction or fantasy, these genres are harder than memoir to do well. Students appreciate having creative freedom, but their characters are often poorly developed, their plots proceed at break-neck pace, and their stories are overdramatized and unrealistic. Plays are even more difficult, with the additional requirement of keeping action located in a limited number of settings, and historical fiction, with its complex interplay of history and story, often leads to pieces of writing that fall short on both counts.

Memoirs lend themselves to better writing because students are writing what they know. They themselves are the main characters of their stories, their friends and family members make up the supporting casts, and the situations and conflicts are things they have personally experienced. True, there is much more to good memoir writing than just putting to paper something that happened to you, but the foundations for creating a believable narrative are firmly in place.

Memoir is also accessible because it is a constantly evolving genre that is not bound by fixed rules. Over the past two decades, memoir writers have been pushing the boundaries of the genre farther and farther. Marjane Satrapi's *Persepolis* (2003) is a graphic novel. Billy Merrell's *Talking in the Dark* (2003) is a collection of poetry. Nick Flynn's *Another Bullshit Night in Suck City* (2004) reads like a piece of experimental fiction. In short, memoir writers, though bound by life experiences, have large amounts of freedom to structure and shape and present those experiences in any way they see fit.

A final point: just as I would argue that students will be more successful writing what they know, so too would I argue that teachers will be more successful teaching a genre of writing that they know how to write well themselves. I confess that I am far more comfortable writing memoir than writing short stories or plays, and that might contribute to my ability to teach this genre effectively and make it so accessible to my students.

4. MEMOIR WRITING PUSHES STUDENTS TO EXPAND THEIR READING HORIZONS

A big part of any writing unit is exposing students to many examples of published writing in that genre. Since most of my students gravitate toward fiction and fantasy, a unit on memoir pushes them to read books they would not necessarily select on their own. This point could be made for many other genres—poetry, historical fiction, biography—but memoir, I would argue, will have wider appeal to a greater number of students. In my eighth-grade class, books like *The Glass Castle* (Walls 2005), *The Burn Journals* (Runyon 2004), *A Long Way Gone* (Beah 2007), *Girl, Interrupted* (Kaysen 1994), and *Bossypants* (Fey 2011) have become as sought after as any fiction or fantasy I have on my shelves. And the fact that all of these books are nonfiction has helped make this term much more palatable to many of my readers, who have long grouped all nonfiction books together under the category "Boring."

Beyond exposing students to a new genre, many contemporary memoirs also help bridge the gap between books written specifically for teenagers and books written for adults, a jump students often face as they move from middle school to high school. Much like the novels *To Kill a Mockingbird* (Lee 1960) and *The Catcher in the Rye* (Salinger 1951), memoirs like the ones mentioned above seem to straddle the worlds of adult and young adult literature and can serve as stepping-stones to the more challenging literature—both fiction and nonfiction—that students will encounter as they progress through school.

5. MEMOIR WRITING CHANGES LIVES

This is a pretty radical statement, but I sincerely believe it to be true. Over the years I have witnessed students confront issues they had previously kept buried and suppressed. I have heard from former students about how their memoirs opened new lines of communication with family members. I have watched students come to see themselves as talented writers for the first time. I have read in their reflections how they have come to realize things about themselves that they never realized before.

Several years ago, the student who wrote *The Rice Bowl* in my eighth-grade classroom found me on Facebook. Via e-mail, I asked her what she remembered about writing her memoir in my class. Here is part of her response:

> I remember being excited about writing my memoir. It was always something
> I wanted to do especially after reading a book about four sisters. (House on
> Mango Street? Garcia girls?) I never had a reason to put things down on paper.
> I remember discussing it with my mom and having her read it over. She cried,
> but it was not crying over sadness. It was crying because she was relieved.
> She was proud that I was able to reflect on it. Before that writing assignment
> I never spoke to anyone in my family about any of it. I had been in therapy
> for a couple of years at that time but I never spoke about it (not even to my
> therapist.). I was afraid of letting my sisters see it in fear that they would feel
> outed. I remember worrying about getting the details right but once I wrote
> it down it did not seem to bother me anymore . . . The final memory I had
> relating to the memoir was receiving the award at graduation on outstanding
> achievement on writing. I never saw myself as a good writer; that was the first
> time I was not self-conscious about what I wrote . . . I know it is long over due

but Thank You so much for everything Mr. Wizner. That memoir assignment led to several other projects in high school and in college.

Shortly after our e-mail exchange, this student invited me to spend a morning at a New York City museum where she works as a book preservationist. Afterward we went to lunch, and she told me that writing the memoir was the stepping-stone to her senior project in high school, interviewing victims of domestic violence, and her decision to study psychology in college. She reported that she had seen her father a few times but did not have a real relationship with him. With her mother and her sisters, however, the bonds had held strong, and they were all still tightly knit together.

"My mother's actually moving in with me and my boyfriend next week," she said. "It's funny. Now my sisters and I are the ones taking care of her."

A student I taught more recently wrote to me early on that she wanted to come out of her shell during eighth grade, to become a more confident and outspoken member of the community. She took steps throughout the year, serving as a tour guide for prospective families, becoming an active participant in the school's drama club, speaking up more in class. But when I met with both her and her mother during parent/teacher conferences, the conversation was awkward and strained, and when I followed up with the student, she seemed reluctant to discuss anything personal.

Then she wrote her memoir, and everything changed. Delving into the most personal aspects of her relationship with her mother and her own insecurities, she ended her memoir, *She's Leaving Home*, as follows:

> All my life I've been keeping things in boxes. Any secrets I had, any memories I didn't want to think about, I packed away and put in storage. But the boxes piled up and closed me in, until I was trapped in a little box of my own. Unable to be social, unable to speak up . . . I didn't want to be like my mom and hide things away. For the first time, I thought everything should be free and out there. I wanted to talk about it.
>
> I guess that's what this memoir is. It's filled with the little things I've never told anyone. The secrets I've kept for so long. It's me taking the first step in unpacking those boxes. Coming to terms with their contents, however ugly they may be. Becoming a more open individual. Symbolically, this memoir is me, leaving home.

One more story: I taught a student, a small but spirited red-haired boy, who had been born with a malformed heart and whose medical issues had followed him through his life, though he never mentioned them, or used them as an excuse. He graduated from our small, sheltered school to a massive high school of four thousand students, where he excelled academically and starred in several of the school's drama productions. In his junior year, the operations and procedures caught up with him. I went to the funeral, moved to see so many of his eighth-grade classmates there. His father spoke passionately at the service, railing against the mistakes and failures of the medical establishment to treat his son, but mostly celebrating his son's courage and zeal for life.

Back at school, I found a copy of this boy's memoir. He had written movingly about his relationship with his father, describing the way his father encouraged him, sometimes through tough love, to achieve great things. I sent a copy of the memoir to his family, and his father wrote me back soon after.

> Thank you so much for sharing David's memoir with me. I will cherish it
> for the rest of my life . . . Again, I want to thank you from the bottom of my heart
> for presenting me with my son's inimitable, beautiful voice from beyond the grave—
> I can think of no greater joy, other than having him back with me.

I looked back at David's memoir recently. What I remembered most clearly from it was the way his father had pushed him to excel in school, and the way David had captured his father's dogged determination not to let him ever give up. But there was another section, more tender in tone, in which David writes about his father taking him to his first baseball game. Reading over this story now, I find that his words resonate with power and meaning in a way that I did not previously fully grasp, but that David undoubtedly did.

> *When we reached Yankee stadium I was overwhelmed by the noise the merchandise*
> *and the sheer excitement of it all. My dad continued to walk at a very fast pace*
> *and I had to run to keep up. My dad laughed and said, "Don't worry, David, if*
> *you can keep up with your dad you can keep up with anyone . . . I didn't really*
> *understand the game but it didn't matter. My dad knew that I wasn't really*

following it so he kept asking me if I wanted to leave but I flatly refused. I planned to stick it out to the very end. And I did.

David's words astound me, as do the words of so many of the students I have taught memoir to over the years. That is why this book is so full of their writing. Their words, more than mine, are the reason I teach memoir.

CHAPTER 2

What's Worth Writing About?

A t the beginning of our memoir unit last year, I asked the students to jot down their feelings about the work we were about to embark upon. Some of the responses were positive, but the majority looked something like this:

I hate memoirs. My mom has never beat me, my dad hasn't walked out on us yet, and I have a generally uninteresting life.

I do not really like writing memoirs. It intimidates me, and the only ones I have written were in elementary school about birthday parties and lemonade stands. I've never written anything deep and personal.

I dislike memoir. I don't think that people of my age have usually had an experience that would make for a good memoir.

I don't like writing about my past. There are a lot of things I don't want to tell anyone.

I am sure that the sentiments of my students are common among adolescents, and the concerns they raise are certainly legitimate. How do you write an interesting memoir if you consider your life uninteresting? Have thirteen-year-old children had enough meaningful experiences and the requisite distance from those experiences to be able to write reflectively about their lives? What if the things most worth writing about are too personal to share?

I confess that my choice to start the unit by reading *The Rice Bowl* exacerbates many of these concerns. Almost none of my students have lived lives so dramatic, and those that have are probably not ready to share their stories. So why do I do it? Why read something that does as much to intimidate my students as to inspire them?

The first reason is that I want to kick off the unit with something that I know everybody will find compelling. Many students have a preconceived notion that memoir is boring, and this piece establishes—without a doubt—that memoir can be every bit as riveting as the best fiction. To see thirty-three thirteen- and fourteen-year-olds sitting completely transfixed as I read a piece of nonfiction written by another student is amazing. They might be intimidated, but at least I have their undivided attention and I have created an unmistakable buzz.

The second reason is that I want the students to understand that this memoir unit is going to be something entirely different from the memoir units they might have done in elementary school when they wrote about birthday parties and lemonade stands. Beyond the length requirement (a minimum of ten typed pages), I expect students to delve more deeply into their lives, to grapple more intensely with who they are, to push out of their comfort zones, to take risks, and to produce writing that feels significant and substantial and maybe even life-changing.

And finally, I know that over the next few days I will share many more student memoirs, most of which are not nearly as dramatic as *The Rice Bowl*, but all of which reflect the kind of thoughtful introspection of the writers' own lives that I expect my current students to engage in.

< 19 >

How Do You Help Students Who Say That Nothing Interesting Has Happened in Their Lives?

Students say this all the time at the beginning of the memoir unit. They say it to me, and they say it to each other, commiserating over the fact that nobody close to them has died, that their divorced parents actually have a good relationship, and that they have never been homeless or hungry or horribly mistreated.

Our job as teachers is to help students discover that they are complex and fascinating individuals; that they do, in fact, have many stories worth telling; and that in the hands of a skilled writer, the ordinary can become extraordinary.

So I tell my students right off the bat that it is okay if they have absolutely no idea what they will write about and that they will have at least two weeks to figure it out. I tell them that during this time we will be looking at lots of memoir excerpts and that I will be showing them different ways to generate memories and to reflect on their lives. I tell them that many of the best memoirs I've gotten over the years have come from students who told me that nothing interesting had happened in their lives.

And for the next two weeks, we engage in a series of writing exercises, and I watch my students unlock their memories and begin to spill fragments of their lives and their identities onto the pages of their notebooks.

How Do You Help Students Negotiate the Balance Between What Is Most Significant and What Is Too Personal to Share?

This is tricky. On the one hand, the point of memoir is to open a window into your life and into who you are, and if you stick to safe and superficial topics you are unlikely to accomplish this, no matter how beautiful the writing. On the other hand, it is clearly not okay to force students, at the risk of a failing grade, to confront their insecurities, expose their family's problems, and make public their most private thoughts. In *Writing a Life,* Katherine Bomer expresses this point eloquently: "There is no final publication or grade or promotion worth causing some students to feel terrified about writing, and we should never force them to go to places inside themselves that they are not ready to meet" (2005, 83).

I have found that most students' reluctance to write about certain things has less to do with their fear of confronting these issues than with their fear that others will read what they have written. Every year, students ask whether they

< 20 >

will have to share their memoirs, whether I will show what they write to their parents, and whether they will get in trouble for sharing past indiscretions that were never caught. I still have on file a letter one of my students wrote me more than a decade ago.

Dear Mr. Wizner,

Right now in my memoir I'm at the point where I just started my first year in Salk. Towards the middle of the year I stole money from one of my teachers but I wasn't caught. To get out of trouble I had to lie through my teeth. I didn't want to tell you because of two reasons.

I didn't want you to trust me any less.

I could get in serious trouble.

I feel it is an important point in my memoir. Without it the memoir would be missing something & it wouldn't be as good a piece. I think for a teacher to get their best work out of their students, the students must be able to trust that whatever they need to say will stay between the two. If they can't then they'll be beating around the bush & the writing won't be the same.

Sincerely,

Ryan

Along these same lines, I have had students who have asked me if they would get in trouble for writing about smoking cigarettes, drinking alcohol, or experimenting with drugs. I have had students ask me if they are allowed to write about other teachers or about classmates they have had issues with. And over and over again, my students have demanded to know who will get to read what they write and if they will be required to share anything they have written with the class.

I think teachers need to weigh their priorities here. Some teachers would argue that if writers are allowed to keep their work confidential, it undermines a key tenet of writing workshop, namely that students work with writing partners or writing groups to provide ongoing feedback and support. And at the end of the unit, when we celebrate the amazing work we have been doing for the past two months, what kind of message are we sending if we make it optional to share? In the words of Katherine Bomer, "Publishing students' memoirs to an audience is perhaps the most important part of the whole process. Writers need authentic response to their products more than they need a grade or even teacher approval" (2005, 31).

Other teachers might feel that getting students to dig deep and grapple with who they are, getting them to write the most powerful, compelling life stories, is the most important thing, and if these stories are too personal to share, then so be it. Teachers themselves can serve as audience and help the students reflect and grow, both as writers and as human beings.

One thing that is nonnegotiable is the students' safety. I explain to my students at the beginning of the unit that teachers are mandated reporters, and if a student writes about being abused, or about having suicidal thoughts, those are things that must be reported to the school guidance counselor, or called in to the appropriate city agency as policy dictates. For issues like smoking or drinking or experimenting with drugs, teachers need to decide if they feel the student is at risk. There is a big difference between an eighth grader who drinks a glass of unattended wine at his friend's Bar Mitzvah and an eighth grader who sneaks out of his East Village apartment when everyone is asleep, meets up with high school kids in Brooklyn to party in an unsupervised apartment, and then comes home by himself on the subway at four in the morning. (These examples are not hypothetical.)

In general, I try to find a middle ground when it comes to balancing all of these competing objectives. I want students to write as openly and honestly as possible, but I want them working together and sharing their writing as well. So I tell students that they can choose their own writing partners and that when they confer, they can focus on the parts of their memoirs they feel most comfortable sharing. Similarly, at the end of the unit celebration, I require students to share only a short excerpt from their final pieces, which, for some students, might be as little as the first two paragraphs.

It's not perfect, and some students end up watering down their work or sharing only the most neutral fragments. But more often than not, something amazing happens during the two months of writing memoir together. Many students who have embarked on their topics only with repeated assurances that they will not have to share anything too personal, end up choosing to share those very sections. Some of this is because they have become so invested in their memoirs and written such powerful and moving stories that they don't want to shortchange themselves at the end of the process. More notably, the shared experience of putting their lives on paper—the many opportunities throughout to share drafts in progress, to reflect on the work, and to learn about each other—forges powerful bonds of community. Everybody is putting him- or herself out there, and there is tremendous respect and admiration showered on the students, who truly expose themselves and open windows into their lives that were previously closed.

Ten Prompts to Help Students Generate Memories and Reflect on Their Lives

During the first two to three weeks of the memoir unit, I offer my students a series of writing prompts and lead them through a series of writing activities to help them unlock their memories and uncover themes worth exploring. Here are ten prompts and activities that I have used over the years:

1. I REMEMBER...

This is perhaps the simplest and most straightforward writing prompt and the one I usually begin with. Ask the students to write the words *I Remember* on the top of a clean page, and then have them list as many things as they can underneath. The memories can be significant or trivial, from a long time ago or from just the other day, serious or funny, about them or about others—in short, whatever pops into their heads. The point of this activity is to make as big a list as possible in the time allotted.

I usually give students about fifteen minutes, and then I have them share at their tables. The sharing is important for a couple of reasons. The first is that the students are excited to share, and if you don't create a time for them to do so, they will do it when they are supposed to be writing. The second is that when students hear each other's memories, it reminds them of things they forgot to write down. I encourage students to jot things down as they listen, and then I give the whole class another ten minutes to write.

After a short break, I ask the students to look over their lists and try to group memories together into broader categories. Many memories, I point out, will fall into several categories. For example, "I remember the time I got bit by a dog" could be in the category "Injuries" but may also fit into the categories "My Relationship with My Father" and "Loss of Innocence."

I tell the students that if they identify categories that many of their memories fall into, they might want to examine those categories in more depth as we move forward.

2. TIME LINES

Time lines are great for a few reasons. They appeal to students who like to organize things chronologically. They combine drawing and writing. And they can take many forms to fit the different ways students might think about their lives. For example, some students might choose to create time lines in which they chunk their lives into eras (preschool, elementary school, middle school). Others might focus on high and low points in their lives and place these events on different planes of the page. Some students might even create a series of time lines to represent different areas of their lives (e.g., home, school, vacations). Have students brainstorm different approaches, and chart their ideas for the class to refer back to.

3. MEMORY MAPPING

Ask students to think of a place associated with many of their memories; the place they choose can be small or large, somewhere they spend time every day or only on special occasions, a fixed space or a place that encompasses more than one location (e.g., the subway, museums, the beach). Then have them make a quick sketch of that place. Tell the students that you are going to provide a series of prompts, and for each one they should jot down a memory that fits the prompt. Stress that they might not have something to write for each prompt, but that they should do as many as they can. Also, tell them to write only a sentence or two for each one, just enough so that they will know what memory they are referring to. Possible prompts might include: a happy memory associated with your place; a sad memory; an embarrassing memory; a memory of getting in trouble; a memory of a significant conversation; a memory of learning something; a memory of being scared; a memory of a fight or an argument; a memory of being alone.

After students have finished identifying a series of memories, you might ask them to select one or two that really stand out and flesh them out into more detailed stories.

4. CASTING THE CHARACTERS IN YOUR LIFE STORY

Imagine your life was a play. List all the characters that would have a part.

This is another simple, straightforward prompt to help students realize how much material they have. Their lists of characters will be vast—family members, family friends, classmates, teachers, neighbors, babysitters, camp counselors, coaches, the guy you see on the bus every day, the list goes on and on. Have students review their lists and put stars next to the people who would have the biggest parts. Have them put checks next to the people who might not have such big parts but whose parts still seem very important for one reason or another. For example, there was a girl named Jennifer I went to camp with one summer when I was about eleven. I hardly spoke to her and I don't remember her last name or exactly what she looked like, but I do remember that she was the first girl I ever had a crush on and I remember the feelings I had as I sat a few rows in front of her on the bus and sneaked peaks in her direction.

As with the "I Remember . . ." prompt, have students look for interesting and illuminating ways to group people together.

5. AREAS OF CONFLICT

Without conflict, there is no story, and so it is essential that students think about the areas of conflict in their lives. These conflicts can be internal or external, large or small, long resolved or ongoing. When I make my list of conflicts from the first thirteen years of my life, I realize that several of the things on my list would have been too embarrassing for me to include at the time. I usually let my students know that when I was in eighth grade, I was incredibly insecure about my weight. I wore clothing that was too big for me, and I hated going swimming because I didn't want anyone to see me without a shirt on. That's easy for me to say now, I tell them, but I would have been incredibly uncomfortable sharing that publicly with my class when I was in eighth grade. I let students know that I'm sure there are some things they're not ready to share because they're right in the middle of them. They need to know that these lists will be private and that I will not force anybody to share.

Again, as with many of the other prompts, I encourage students to select one or two conflicts that seem especially significant and spend some time writing about them in more depth.

< 25 >

6. THEMATIC PROMPTS

Everybody has a different story, but there are certain themes that are universal. Three interrelated themes that I think every young memoir writer should grapple with are growing up, identity, and change. There are many ways to get students to reflect on these themes. You can do freewrites based on broad questions (Who am I? How am I different now from when I was younger? What are all the ways my life has changed since I was little?). You can have students respond to the following prompt in as many ways as possible.

I used to be _____, but now I am
_____.

Or you can combine this work with one of the other prompts. For example, students might create thematic time lines, in which they trace different kinds of changes they have experienced during their lives.

7. MY CRAZY/UNUSUAL/DYSFUNCTIONAL FAMILY

So much of who we are, so much of our life experience, is inextricably tied up with the lives and personalities of our family members. Ask students to talk about who has weird parents, annoying siblings, crazy relatives, and they'll be off and running. Push students to think about what makes their family unique. I might ask, How is your family different from the families of your friends? Are there certain rituals your family has? What are the areas of tension and conflict in your home? What's something about your family that you love? What's something you wish you could change?

Here are some other questions to get students writing:

What things make your family interesting/different/unusual/complicated? How have these things affected your life and/or influenced you?

Tell me about your parents. What has it been like growing up with them? What has been good? What has been challenging?

Tell me about your siblings. What has it been like growing up with them? What has been good? What has been challenging? If you don't have siblings, how has that affected your life? What has been good or challenging?

Are your parents divorced or separated? What happened? How did it affect your life?

How does your family operate? What are the rules? What are the rituals? What are the dynamics of interactions with one another?

How have your relationships with your family members changed as you've grown older?

What are some things you understand about your family or any of your family members that you did not understand when you were younger?

8. PASSIONS/HOBBIES/OBSESSIONS

Over the course of your lifetime, what are the different things you have been passionate about?

Before eighth grade, my passions included Hot Wheels cars, superheroes, baseball cards, foosball, and Greek mythology. Three decades later, I still have vivid memories around each of these interests and could write compellingly about their significance during my childhood. When students begin to write about the things they are most passionate about, they often open a window into their world and into who they are or once were.

9. DIFFERENT WORLDS, DIFFERENT SELVES

My mother tells the story that when she would meet with my nursery school teachers, they would always gush about how well behaved I was, how nice I was to the other children, how helpful and cooperative and gentle and kind. This must have come as quite a shock to her the first time she heard it, considering the fact that she once brought my brother and me to the pediatrician and claimed there must be something wrong with us because we acted like wild animals.

Adolescents, even more so than toddlers, occupy several different worlds. (This is especially true today with the advent of Facebook and other online communities.) Having students write about the different worlds they occupy is a great way to get them thinking about their different selves and to grapple with the question, Who am I?

This prompt has been especially useful for students struggling with their cultural identities. Many of my students have parents who were born in another country, do not speak English, and are not nearly as assimilated as their children. These students often write powerfully about the ways in which they struggle to fit into the very different worlds of home and school. Similarly, I have had students over the years use this prompt as a springboard to write memoirs about the racial, religious, and sexual identity struggles they have experienced.

10. SIGNIFICANT OBJECTS/ARTIFACTS

Walk around your room or your house. Look at all of your stuff. Which objects hold the most meaning? Write about those objects and why they are so significant. What are the memories that you associate with them? What larger stories and themes spring from your recollections?

I still have my intramural basketball t-shirt from when I was a senior in high school more than twenty-five years ago. It is maroon, with a white basketball on the front, and the letters WIZ on the back. It is completely tattered now, the lettering has peeled away, and I have not worn it in more than a decade. But I'm not quite ready to throw it out. I see it in my closet, and I think back to that year when I was the captain of my team, when we pulled off a shocking playoff upset of the league's number one seed and then came within one basket of winning the school championship. I won the intramural basketball league award that year and was among the students honored during assembly one morning. It was a beautiful thing, in what was otherwise a rather depressing time. I look back at high school, and I think about how I never had a close group of friends, how I never kissed a girl, how I never really got involved in school life, but then I remember how I would put on that shirt, and the socially awkward Jake Wizner would become, for a short time at least, the Wiz.

✳   ✳   ✳   ✳   ✳

Two final thoughts in regard to the work I do with writing prompts that actually have larger implications in terms of teaching writing in general:

1. **Different things work for different writers.**
   I stress to my students over and over again that not all of the prompts will be useful to everyone. I usually ask them to try out everything we do and tell them not to worry if some of the prompts seem like dead ends. I do recognize the contradiction in saying that different things work for different writers and then asking all my students to go through the process of writing off a series of teacher-generated prompts. In general, the students seem to embrace the process, especially since I keep the

prompts as open-ended as possible and invite my students to respond in any way that makes sense to them.

2. **Do the work you're asking the students to do.**

There are several reasons why this is important. It ensures that anything you ask students to do, you have already tried out and found worthwhile. It provides models for the students to use as they try out the prompts themselves. It makes you part of the community of writers. And it encourages the kind of trusting environment you need for memoir work by revealing personal (though not too personal) details from your own life. When I am doing these prompts, I situate myself in eighth grade because I want my experience to reflect as closely as possible the experience of my students, and I want to cut off the excuse that I have an unfair advantage because I've lived so much longer. Of course I do have an unfair advantage, because my age allows me to write about adolescent issues and insecurities from a much safer place than that afforded my students, but it also allows me to say to my students, I know what it is to be thirteen. I was overweight and insecure around girls and not nearly as popular as my brother and scared about going to high school. But the good news is that it all turns out okay in the end. Just look at how cool I am now.

CHAPTER 3

The Reading-
Writing
Connection

It seems like a strange thing for an eleven-year-old to be doing, but I'd begun
reading fantasy novels faster than people were pumping them out. First the Lord
of the Rings trilogy, then Cornelia Funke and so on. I read the Pendragon books
and His Dark Materials. I was absolutely infatuated with the genre. I could
practically talk in Elfish and knew the lands of Middle Earth and Narnia better
than the back of my hand. It was inevitable that I would write one myself.

—*One More Page* (Jeremy's eighth-grade memoir)

The principal at my school tells a story about how she arrived at college and got a poor grade on her first lab report. She was distraught, accustomed as she was to receiving only top marks on all of her work. The professor told the class that if they wanted to learn how to write lab reports correctly, some "model" papers were available for them to look at, and when my principal began to read through them, it was if a curtain had been lifted from her eyes. "I had never really learned to write a lab report in high school," she said. "Just studying those papers taught me more about science writing than I had learned in the past four years."

This is a dangerous story for a writing teacher to be sharing because it suggests that developing writers need examples of good writing more than they

< 30 >

need human teachers. Certainly, scores of published authors have pointed to their reading, rather than to their teachers, as the key to improving their craft. "There are many rules of good writing," Stephen Ambrose remarks, "but the best way to find them is to be a good reader" (2003, 188). F. Scott Fitzgerald echoes the sentiment: "A good style simply doesn't form unless you absorb half a dozen top flight authors every year" (1995, 455). Even Steven Spielberg, who mastered writing of a different sort, emphasizes the reading-writing connection: "Only a generation of readers will spawn a generation of writers" (1986).

Katherine Bomer, who is both a writer and a teacher, notes that "everything a writer needs to know about how to write can be found in the texts that exemplify the genre" (2005, 42). This does not make teachers irrelevant, however. Our job as teachers, she points out, is to expose students to these mentor texts and to guide them in how to use these texts as instruction manuals in the art of writing—to help students read with the eyes of writers.

Clearly, then, a huge part of teaching students to write well in any genre is to make sure they read widely in the genre they are attempting. During the memoir unit, students read memoirs individually, in book clubs, and as a whole class. They study memoirs written by their peers, by past eighth graders, and by published authors. And these mentor texts—*plus the discussions and lessons that stem from them*—are instrumental in guiding the students as they grapple with what to write about and how to do it most effectively.

*   *   *

You might have noticed that the writing activities I described in the previous chapter seem to be focused considerably more on generating content than on developing craft. I confess that in the first two weeks of our memoir study, my primary objective is to help students nail down *what* they want to write about, and I am far less concerned with teaching them *how* to write about these topics most effectively. But even if I draw a line between lessons in content and lessons in craft, there is still a very pronounced reading-writing connection throughout the unit. From the first day, we are looking at student models to help us reach a definition of what memoir is and what memoir is not. We are examining in these models the many possible things students can choose to write about, the different structures and tones memoirs can take, and the reasons why some memoirs are more compelling than others. Hand in hand with working through the prompts

I described in the previous chapter are multiple opportunities to read and discuss finished memoirs from past students that originated from those particular prompts. In fact, most students have read more than a dozen of these (each one at least ten pages long) before they settle on what they themselves wish to write about.

While most teachers would agree that immersion in the genre is a key component to any writing unit, the ways we both choose and use mentor texts can vary considerably. For example, I tend to use mostly student models in the early weeks when students are trying to figure out what to write about. Later, when I start to focus on elements of craft, I revisit these memoirs, looking at them through a different lens, and I pull in examples from published memoirs by professional writers.

Many teachers of memoir writing take a different approach, showing how content and craft go hand in hand. From the beginning, they are providing models of beautiful memoir writing, examining the craft of these pieces with their students, and then asking the students to write short pieces of their own using the published models as mentor texts.

Katherine Bomer (2005) immerses her students in beautiful memoir writing throughout the unit. During the week in which students are generating memories in their notebooks, she is sharing excerpts from many published authors as prompts for the students' own exploratory writing. She describes an activity very similar to the "I Remember . . ." activity listed in the previous chapter, but before having students launch into their freewriting, she reads them an excerpt from Paul Auster's *The Invention of Solitude* (1982), in which the author begins each sentence with the words, *He remembers.* She does not ask them to imitate Auster's style, but she is, indirectly at least, exposing students to beautiful craft, even if her primary goal in this activity is to generate ideas.

In their book *New Directions in Teaching Memoir*, Dawn Latta Kirby and Dan Kirby suggest that students write many short exploratory pieces (called "spider" pieces, alluding to the way spiders throw out thread after thread until one attaches securely and becomes the anchor around which the remainder of the web is woven). These pieces arise from prompts designed to get students to zero in on different aspects of their lives and identities, but before writing each piece, students examine models and discuss craft. For a spider piece about students' own names, for example, Kirby and Kirby show several published excerpts and invite students to notice "what the author tells us about names in the piece, how the names are important, whether the names are liked or disliked by those who hold them, the voice employed by each narrator—child's voice, adult-looking-back-in-time voice, third-person omniscient detached voice—vocabulary and other relevant writer's craft features of the piece" (2007, 36).

In this chapter, I show some of the different ways I use mentor texts in my classroom during the memoir unit, and how my students' reading shapes their writing.

Matching Students to Texts That Inspire Them to Write

Richie was struggling with his memoir. A bright boy who rarely worked up to his potential, he had gotten poor grades and been in a fair share of trouble throughout middle school. I recommended Tobias Wolff's *This Boy's Life* (1989), thinking that he would really connect with the central character, a boy who was very much like Richie in many ways. Sure enough, Richie devoured the book, saying it was one of the best he had ever read.

It turned out that there were more similarities in the two boys' stories than I had anticipated, something I learned when Richie suddenly took off with his memoir. In particular, the section in which Tobias Wolff reinvents himself to be accepted into boarding school spoke directly to Richie's own experiences in applying to private high schools earlier in the year. Richie, much like the author, had less than stellar transcripts but came to believe that he belonged in the rarified world of private schools. He describes his first visit to a private school as follows:

> *The building was huge and full of extra things that I never could have imagined in my school. Plasma screen TVs showing pictures of smiling faces, and couches all around for kids to sit and read in . . . I had never seen any gym as big as this one; it had a high ropes course, a weight room, and the normal basketball court.*
>
> *"What do you think?" my mom asked me.*
>
> *I couldn't respond, I was so breath-taken by this gym that I think right then and there my whole nasty opinion about high school changed . . . When we left the building, I couldn't control the happiness I was feeling.*

Tobias Wolff, longing to be accepted into boarding school, describes how he forged his letters of recommendation to give himself a fighting chance:

The words came as easily as if someone were breathing them into my
ear. I felt full of things that had to be said, full of stifled truth . . .
I believed in some sense not factually verifiable I was a straight-A
student. In the same way I believed I was an Eagle Scout, and a
powerful swimmer, and a boy of integrity . . . I wrote without heat
or hyperbole, in the words my teachers would have used if they had
known me as I knew myself. (1989, 213–214)

Richie also recognizes that he needs to reinvent himself, but he is far less comfortable doing so and grapples with whether the things he says about himself
are, on some level, actually true.

> *I hated dressing up for this "part" I was playing. I say "part" because I thought it*
> *was all fake, I thought that half the things I was saying about myself were untrue,*
> *but of course they weren't. Mainly because some of the things I was saying I had*
> *no idea were true . . . I got along with all of my interviewers and I found that*
> *I had, as some people say, "mastered the art" of interviews. Basically what that*
> *means is I can play any part that is needed. For example if I was applying to a*
> *Catholic school, I could be "very religious."*

Reading *This Boy's Life* informed so much of Richie's memoir-writing experience,
providing him with inspiration for a topic, helping him uncover his theme, and
motivating him to do far and away the best work he had done all year. The simple
act of matching him to a memoir that spoke so directly to his experiences and to
his sense of self had a profound effect on the writer he became during the unit.

✽   ✽   ✽

Alyssa did not need a mentor text for inspiration. She needed a mentor text to
show her how to write a memoir in poetry form.

Early in the unit Alyssa made the decision to write about the death of her
father. As she began to write, she found that her thoughts and feelings were
emerging in fragments of language and as a series of images more suited to
poetry than to prose. Having never seen a poetry memoir, however, she shied
away from this genre and ended up writing a draft that was begging to break
free from its prosaic constraints.

I suggested she commit herself to writing her memoir as poetry and gave her Billy Merrell's *Talking in the Dark* (2003) to show her what that might look like. She came to see that a series of poems could work together to tell a story in much the same way as her very brief chapters of prose. And she embraced the challenges of trimming excess language, using line breaks to create rhythm and meaning, and writing poems that enhanced each other, but could also stand very much on their own. Here is a poem from her memoir *The Evanescent Girl*.

IT'S THE WINGS
They sit under the jungle gym
Fairy doll in hand.
Across from her sits
A small
Frail girl with an inaudible voice
Scattered around her lie the bodies
Of plastic worlds

With a leaf,
Moss,
Half a walnut shell
And a few sticks
On her back is a pair of
Shiny
White
Fairy wings.
Convinced that there is something magical,
That we cannot see but is all around us,
And she still believes

(Thank you third grade self.)

Here is the next poem in the memoir. Notice how each poem captures a moment in time, and how the final lines of the first poem are all the more poignant when read in conjunction with the second poem.

THE HOSPITAL
White walls surround her
That only add
To the odd feeling
Of the fluorescent lights beating
Down on her head.
There is no sun,
Only chairs
And the thin wall
Separating her from her father.
Her father
A man
Who appears to have been
Strong willed
Until he was confined
To the small bed
On which he lies
Hooked up to a machine
And unable to speak
His eyes are closed,
Thinner than he ever was,
He looks...
Weak,
Feeble even.
She digs her head deeper in the book,
Separating her from the other people in the room,
From the thoughts that haunt her.
It doesn't matter
What the words say,
It's the only thing she has.
She clings on to the book as if
It was her father's life.
On a thread
She can't help but take a deep shaky breath
Breathing is the only thing keeping her from

Crying
All she can do is keep breathing.

Reading and rereading Billy Merrell's memoir was guidance and inspiration enough for Alyssa to recast her memoir in poetry form and to transform a powerful and moving piece of writing into a genuine work of art.

Imitating Specific Techniques of Craft

The act of matching students to mentor texts is one way to promote the reading-writing connection in a classroom. But teaching students how to examine those texts for specific techniques of craft is equally important. Throughout the memoir unit, my students and I seek out writing that thrills us, put words to what it is that the authors are doing, and then imitate the passages we have selected. Here are some techniques of craft we uncover in our reading.

FIGURATIVE LANGUAGE

One memoir that some of my students choose to read is Maya Angelou's *I Know Why the Caged Bird Sings* (1997). Maya Angelou uses figurative language—similes and metaphors in particular—as effectively as any writer I have encountered. In just the opening few pages of *I Know Why the Caged Bird Sings*, she illuminates the pain and shame of her childhood with images that are vivid, evocative, and spot-on.

> 'What you looking at me for? I didn't come to stay . . .'
> . . . The truth of the statement was like a wadded-up handkerchief,
> sopping wet in my fists, and the sooner they accepted it the quicker I
> could let my hands open and the air would cool my palms.
>
> The dress I wore was lavender taffeta, and each time I breathed it
> rustled, and now that I was sucking in air to breathe out shame it
> sounded like crepe paper on the back of hearses.
>
> The giggles hung in the air like melting clouds that were waiting to
> rain on me.

I tried to hold, to squeeze it back, to keep it from speeding, but when
I reached the church porch I knew I'd have to let it go, or it would
probably run right back up to my head and my poor head would burst
like a dropped watermelon, and all the brains and spit and tongue and
eyes would roll all over the place.

If growing up is painful for the Southern Black girl, being aware of
her displacement is the rust on the razor that threatens the throat.
It is an unnecessary insult. (1997, 1–4)

We talk about how Maya Angelou uses language to help us visualize her feelings,
almost as if she were taking an abstract idea and painting a picture of what it
might look like. We talk about how her similes and metaphors provide new ways
of looking at the world, how they manage to be both unexpected and brimming
with truth. And we look for places in our memoirs where we can experiment
with similes and metaphors to make our writing more interesting and to convey
our ideas in new and original ways.

Ethan is writing about his experience witnessing his father being arrested.
He is grappling with how to convey the confusion, distress, and sadness he felt,
as well as the sense that a piece of him was gone. The simile he comes up with
helps capture these feelings brilliantly.

Neither of them [my aunt or my cousin] could look me directly in the eyes. Why?
What had I done? Was it my fault? These questions floated around my mind like
dead fish in a fish tank . . .

Willa is describing her grandparents' apartment in Hong Kong. Look at how her
similes evoke both the decay and the majesty of old age.

The paint on the walls is peeling from the cracks like the ice cracking on the frozen
river. The wooden closet stands next to me like an old tree in the forest, containing
a history of the past, with pictures and antiques and special things.

Vivian creates an image that is both totally original and totally recognizable to
illustrate the fights between her mother and her grandmother.

*I've always pictured them both on stage, singing at an opera or something. You
know the female Vikings with the helmets with the horns sticking out on each side.
They would just go on without having to take a breath or anything.*

SECOND-PERSON PERSPECTIVE

Memoirs, by definition, are first-person accounts. It is rare, therefore, when a
memoir writer shifts from a first-person voice and writes from a different perspective. In *First French Kiss*, Adam Bagdasarian writes primarily from a first-person perspective, but occasionally he shifts to a second-person perspective, most
notably in the story in which he learns that his father has died.

> You wake up and make yourself breakfast. You read the Sunday comics
> and eat with your brother and sister. It's ten o'clock. Your mother is in
> bed because she doesn't feel well. She has the flu. You mention to your
> brother and sister how nice it is that Pop is sleeping late. Usually he's
> downstairs before anyone. He must be pretty tired. (2002, 122)

Second person is an unusual perspective in writing—most often identified with
those old choose-your-own-adventure books—and my students and I discuss why
the author might choose to write several of his stories in this second-person voice.

"It makes it feel like you are the one experiencing what is happening," one
student says. "So it's more powerful."

Another student offers a different interpretation. "The whole thing doesn't feel
real to him. That's why he switches away from the first-person voice. It's like even
though these things are happening, he feels somehow disconnected from it all."

After reading this section, some of my students decide to experiment with
second-person perspective in their writing. Here, Clarissa uses this perspective
extremely effectively to open her memoir.

*You're a young child, and so far you believe your life is perfect. You're getting what
you want and you're being loved. Until one night you wake up from your sleep
to the sound of screaming and shouting coming from your parents' mouths. You
get scared and don't know what's going on, so you cover your ears and scream,
hoping that whatever it is they are doing will just stop and they will notice you
and everything will turn back to the way it was. But when that doesn't work you*

hug them and they notice and your mom says, Go to your room now," but your father says, "Hand me the diamond bracelet." Your mom yells, "No don't do it just keep it on." Then you have your dad yelling at you asking you for the diamond bracelet and you hesitate, not knowing who to listen to and all of a sudden your dad starts to tug at the bracelet on your wrist but you fight back not wanting to give it to him because your aunt made it for you and you love it, but he pulls and pulls and it starts to hurt but you don't want him to have it. All of a sudden your mom watching all of this says, "Let him have it, just let go," and you listen and your dad yanks it off of you and walks out of the apartment with it in his hands. You don't want him to have it and you don't want him to go so you walk to the door hoping he isn't gone yet and stick your hand right in the area where the door slams shut which it does, right on your finger. Luckily there is a ring there so all it does is break the ring and make your finger swollen. You yell and holler because of the pain and see your father walking down the stairs without even looking back. Your mom drags you toward the bathroom and places your finger under cold water for a long time making it feel better. When your finger doesn't hurt as much, she dries it off and hugs you and you ask her, "Why did daddy take my bracelet?" and she says, "He's going to sell it." You don't understand and you run straight to your room and start to cry, cry so much you're exhausted and end up falling asleep . . .

Leila describes cutting herself, but the second-person voice makes it seem more like an explanation of the process than the re-creation of a specific memory. Still, her pain and emotion gush out, drawing us in and making us a part of everything she is describing. We are both spectators and participants, horrified by and complicit in the pain she is feeling.

You slide the razor sideways across your leg so it will make a clean, smooth cut. It doesn't hurt at first. At first, you don't even see it. Then the blood rises to the surface and the blood begins to flow. You want the control you've never had over your life. You want to say something! You have to say something! You want to scream out what is happening to you and what you are feeling! You want to cry and scream and make a scene and explode the world twenty-six times! You slam your hand on the side of the bathtub! It throbs. You want to make someone look at you! Won't somebody listen to you? You can't stay silent! You need someone to look at you and listen to you and talk to you, but nobody gives a flying fuck! You are fighting everything and running from it at the same time. Intense anger, intense fear—they are one. The tears streaming down your cheek feel acidic—they burn holes in your face, your body, your heart. Nobody cares. Even you. You're FAT, Rude, Stupid, Pitiful. Pathetic. You have no friends now, and your grandmother's gone. And look at your thighs: bratwurst with stretch marks. Flabby. Disgusting. And your hips and waist: if you cut yourself in half you might look normal! You are fighting everything and running from it at the same time. Intense anger, intense fear—

They are one.

And then you just lie back and let the sting in your leg consume you because it's ten times better than what you were feeling three seconds ago.

HYBERBOLE

Writers often include exaggerated statements or details for emphasis or effect. It is one way they give their writing voice and make their words come alive on the page. Look at this passage from *First French Kiss* in which the author describes kissing Maggie Mann when the two were in sixth grade.

> I took my place in the center of the circle and looked at Maggie. It was a smoldering, masterful look that caused every girl in the room to sigh and begin whispering . . . Maggie stood, as though summoned by a sublime and irresistible fate, and floated across the floor toward me. We gazed at each other a moment, then kissed a lyrical, transportational kiss that astonished our friends, confounded our enemies, and silenced the room in general. (Bagdasarian 2002, 6)

Nathan experiments with this technique when writing about the time his toilet overflowed. Notice how his use of over-the-top language transforms this memory into something truly fabulous and funny, and how his comic voice really carries the scene.

Oh my gosh, how could I stop it? The water was starting to go on my bathroom floor . . . Suddenly a solution to my problem passed my eyes. It was red and big with a long wooden handle; its bright magnificent light shined in my eyes. It was the great plunger. I picked it up and felt a strong power. I dipped the plunger in the

< 41 >

*toilet flowing with yellow liquid and I pushed it into the great black hole of the
toilet, the toilet's mouth. I pushed and pulled the plunger several times till finally
the irritating noise of the toilet started to calm down. The toilet finally died and the
bathroom was quiet now. The only thing you could hear were the drops of water
dripping into the new clear fresh toilet water. I felt like a medieval knight who
had just killed a raging dragon. I stood in the bathroom looking at the mess on
the floor. I was standing on my own urine. I looked down at the monster that had
caused it and I noticed that there was a Barbie doll head floating through the clear
water in the toilet. This must have caused the flood. Who would have done such
a stupid thing? My four-year-old sister! That idiot! How could she do something
like this, I moaned. She must have dropped it or something after taking a bath last
night, I thought. Boy, would she get it. She had to suffer.*

CRAFT LESSONS ARE EVERYWHERE

If we read with an eye to craft, there is almost no limit to the techniques we can
uncover. Look at how Tobias Wolff starts this chapter in *This Boy's Life*.

> Marian and Kathy and my mother decided to rent a house together.
> My mother offered to find the house, and so she did. It was the most
> scabrous eyesore in West Seattle. Paint hung in strips off the sides, the
> bare wood weathered to a gray, antlerish sheen. The yard was knee-
> high in weeds. The sagging eaves had been propped up with long
> planks, and the front steps were rotted through. To get inside you
> had to go around to the back door. Behind the house was a partly
> collapsed barn that little kids liked to sneak into, drawn there by the
> chance to play with broken glass and rusty tools.
> My mother took it on the spot. (1989, 57)

The last line is fabulous in the way it undercuts all our expectations, but it only
works because Wolff has described the awfulness of the house in such vivid detail.

Or look at what Adam Bagdasarian does in *First French Kiss*. In one story
entitled "Popularity," he compares the social hierarchy among his classmates to
that of a kingdom.

> I gazed at Sean and the rest of the popular boys in bewildered
> admiration. It seemed like only yesterday that we had all played
> kickball, dodgeball, and basketball together; and then one morning
> I awoke to find that this happy democracy had devolved into a
> monarchy of kings and queens, dukes and duchesses, lords and ladies.
> It did not take a genius to know that, upon the continent of this
> playground, the two Allans and I were stableboys. (2002, 45)

There are several possible craft lessons that emerge from this short passage. There is Bagdasarian's use of an extended metaphor. There is his use of hyperbole, a technique we saw him employ earlier in describing his kiss. There is the lovely parallel structure when he writes of the playground democracy devolving into "a monarchy of kings and queens, dukes and duchesses, lords and ladies." And then there is also the way that the author brilliantly returns to his metaphor in a later story, after he himself has become popular and is about to be knocked off his perch.

> Strangely, I felt not like a boy on his way to a fight but like a king on
> his way to the gallows. These were not my classmates before me but
> peasants in revolt. My wife had already been beheaded, my children
> sold for horses, my servants set free. (2002, 67)

Some of these techniques might be too challenging for students to incorporate into their memoirs, but it is still worthwhile for them to see the many ways authors manipulate language to create beautiful writing.

An Easy and Effective Strategy to Help Students Read with the Eye of a Writer

Throughout the memoir unit, students read published memoirs that serve as mentor texts and use their reading notebooks to record what they are learning about content and craft. The most effective strategy I have found to get students to think about craft and to learn from other writers is copy-change.

I first encountered copy-change in a graduate-level writing class. Our teacher, a professional writer, gave us a collection of some of his favorite passages and asked us to choose one of them to imitate. We could write about whatever we pleased, he said, but we must capture the voice and the rhythm of the passage, and whatever else it was that made the passage sing.

With my students, I have provided a bit more scaffolding for this work. Very early in the year, long before we begin the memoir unit, I show my students these four sentences:

1. He is hungry, tired, cold, and alone.

2. He is hungry, tired, cold, alone.

3. He is hungry and tired and cold and alone.

4. He is hungry and tired, cold and alone.

We study the sentences, noting what is different about each one, and then I ask my students to write their own series of four sentences modeled exactly after the four I have shown them. This is how I introduce the idea of copy-change.

We then move on to a more interesting and complex sentence, like this one by George Garrett, from his story "The Last of the Spanish Blood":

> He was one of the barefooted, shambling, overage, shaggy-haired, snaggletoothed, dulleyed cracker boys who always came to school in overalls and never took a bath. (Garrett 1960)

Before I ask students to imitate this sentence, we dissect it, noting all the things the author does to make it so wonderful. It's not enough for students to notice that he uses a lot of adjectives. I want them to see exactly how many he uses, because it's the large number that creates some of the effect. I want them to note, also, how wonderfully descriptive each adjective is, that the author does not use adjectives like, *dumb* or *ugly* or *old*. We look at the effect created by the first five words, how those words set up the expectation that he is describing a certain kind of person that we might recognize. We look at the juxtaposition of antonyms near the end of the sentence—"who always . . . and never."

I show them my own imitation, pointing out how I have tried to capture all the elements we have identified.

She was one of the overweight, red-haired, face-lifted, name-dropping, canasta-playing Miami Beach grandmothers who always called people "darling" and never had a nice thing to say.

And then I set my students loose.

By the time we get to the memoir unit, the students have had a fair amount of practice with copy-change. As they read published memoirs, I ask them regularly to engage in this work. Here are the directions I give them and an example of what the finished work looks like.

a. Identify a passage that stands out to you for some reason. Copy (or photocopy and insert) the passage into your notebook, and include the page number.

b. Write a few sentences explaining why you chose the passage. Be specific.

c. Imitate the passage using content from your own life.

Example:

a. (From *First French Kiss*)

Linda Lieban was an artist, a free spirit, a bohemian who played the flute in the park, drew pictures of winged horses and naked nymphs, and signed these drawings with the blood from her own pricked finger. She was someone, we all knew, who was destined to go to New York, dance on tabletops, pose naked for struggling artists, and rally the masses to riot. (Bagdasarian 2002, 50)

b. I love how Adam Bagdasarian brings this character to life in one short paragraph. His description is over-the-top and exaggerated (the literary term is hyperbole), but it works to highlight the fact that this girl was really a free spirit. The free spirit also comes alive in the sentence structure, with sentences that run long, building momentum as they go.

c. (My Imitation)

My younger brother was a whiz kid, an intellectual prodigy, a genius who won political debates with adults, read Shakespeare for fun, and forced teachers to redesign their curriculum for him. He was someone, my parents claimed, who would one day go to Harvard, argue cases in front of the Supreme Court, win a Pulitzer Prize, and dazzle foreign dignitaries with his intellect and wit.

That's it. But if students do this regularly—choose passages they love, reflect on what makes them great, and imitate them—the effect on their writing is profound.

Some Final Thoughts

William Zinsser describes craft as "carpentry." He writes: "Good memoirs are a careful act of construction. We like to think that an interesting life will simply fall into place on the page. It won't ... Memoir writers must manufacture a text, imposing narrative order on a jumble of half-remembered events" (1987, 6). Annie Dillard holds craft equal to content when she says, "I admire artists who succeed in dividing my attention more or less evenly between the world of their books and the art of their books" (1987, 158).

How do we learn to construct our texts effectively? How do we learn to weave language in truly artistic ways? We work to create a culture in which we read with the eyes of writers and are as attentive to the nuances of craft as we are to the choices of content. For some people this comes naturally. My father, for example, often becomes totally absorbed in books that I have found to be ponderously slow. "I don't read for plot," he tells me. "I read for beautiful writing."

I try to capture this sentiment—albeit a bit more crudely—through the character of Mr. Parke in my first novel, *Spanking Shakespeare* (2007). Whenever this English teacher comes across writing that thrills him, he cries out, "I'd give my left testicle to write a sentence like that!"

Perhaps my favorite quote comes from the Canadian writer W.P. Kinsella, best known for his novel *Shoeless Joe* (1982), which was adapted into the movie *Field of Dreams*. His words encapsulate the reading-writing connection beautifully, and I keep them posted in my classroom throughout the year. "Read! Read! Read! And then read some more. When you find something that thrills you, take it apart paragraph by paragraph, line by line, word by word, to see what made it so wonderful. Then use those tricks the next time you write."

< 46 >

CHAPTER 4

Fact and Truth

Art is the lie that tells the truth.

—Pablo Picasso

My dad always wanted to make sure that my childhood and my brother's would be nothing like his own. His own father had never introduced him to sports so Dad began playing catch with us when we were two and three and even started propping us up in his bed at night to watch baseball and football games on TV. His father had never taken him skiing or hiking so Dad filled our early childhood with a series of outdoor excursions. In the winter, Dad would drive us across Connecticut to ski at Powder Ridge and would patiently pull my brother and me up a small practice hill because we were too small to ride the chairlift. In warmer weather, we would set off for Westwood Trails in Guilford for long afternoons of hiking. Dad would help me across the ledges and down into the cave, always catching me as I jumped into his outstretched arms.

I was five, maybe six, and Dad and I were on our first outing of the season to Edgewood Park. It was a breezy Saturday afternoon, green sweater weather for my dad, grey hooded sweatshirt weather for me. Buckled in the front seat, I could barely contain my excitement. Next to me, my father was tremendous. I had memorized his height—six foot three—and by virtue of this staggering statistic he was the greatest person I knew.

As my dad parked the car and turned off the motor, I pushed through the door and ran off ahead of him toward the swings in the playground. Twenty feet short I pulled up. A large brown dog was stretched out in front of the swings, regarding *me with wary interest. He did not move his body but he kept his head raised and his eyes fixed on me. I turned back to my father, who was just settling down on a nearby bench.*

"Go ahead," he called. "The dog won't bother you."

It was true that the dog seemed calm enough. If he were dangerous, wouldn't he be on a leash? Wouldn't he have barked at me by now? I took a few steps forward and then lost my resolve. Again I looked back at my father. "What if he bites me?"

"He's not gonna bite you. Just walk over to the swing and he'll move away. If you hold your hand out and let him sniff it, he'll probably want you to pet him."

I took a few tentative steps forward, holding my hand out as my father had suggested. "Nice doggy," I whispered. "Nice doggy."

Suddenly, the dog jumped to his feet, released a fierce growl, and bit me on the leg. I screamed, more from shock than from pain, and crumpled in a heap on the ground. In a blur, I saw my father rush past me in mad pursuit of the fleeing dog. Words that I had never before heard him utter flew in a torrent from his mouth. Indeed, someone watching the scene might well have wondered which of the two, dog or dad, was the rabid one.

Then he was beside me, asking if I was all right, apologizing, pressing my shaking body against his own.

"You said he wouldn't bite me," I stammered.

"Shhh. Shhh. It's okay," my father murmured soothingly. "You'll be okay. You'll be alright."

I continued crying even though my leg did not hurt.

A woman who had witnessed the scene offered to call the pound and walked off in the direction of the nearest pay phone. I pulled the hood of my sweatshirt around and wiped away the leftover tears. Then we waited for what seemed like forever for the people from the pound to arrive.

The sun was starting to go down, and as my father and I walked hand in hand from the park, I stared at the distorted sizes of our fleeting shadows.

❖   ❖   ❖

I wrote this story when I was in high school and rediscovered it about a decade later when I started teaching memoir writing to my eighth graders. One thing that strikes me about this piece is how much of it I must have made up. That's not to say that the piece is a work of fiction. It's just that a lot of what I wrote is probably not factually accurate. I'm sure I guessed at how old I was; I know I couldn't have remembered any of the conversations I had with my father; and I definitely invented the whole thing about our shadows. In fact, the only thing I can say with certainty is that a dog bit me at Edgewood Park when I was a young child, and that I was with my father when it happened. Still, even though my story might not be factually accurate, it is unquestionably truthful, or at least it was truthful when I wrote it. And truth, not fact, lies at the heart of writing memoir.

What Is the Difference Between Fact and Truth?

I ask my students this question in regard to memoir writing and get a range of interesting responses. "Facts are what happened," one student says. "Truth is your interpretation of what happened." Another student suggests, "Truth is like facts plus emotion." A third student has a different take. "Facts are things that can be proven. Truth is different for everybody."

Indeed, not only is truth different for everybody—witness the different ways people remember the same event—but truth is also different for each of us individually at different times in our lives. In other words, we are constantly reinterpreting the things we have seen and experienced, so our understanding of what is true is always evolving.

Take the story with the dog. For many years I believed that the significance of the incident was in the fact that my father had failed to keep me safe. I remembered this as being the first time that I realized that my father was not some all-powerful, all-knowing superhero, who could always be trusted. It was the first incident that I could remember that caused me to redefine my father and reevaluate our relationship. This, undoubtedly, was what I was trying to convey with the "distorted sizes" of our shadows.

Now that I am a father with two daughters who are about the same age as I was when the incident occurred, I am starting to think about this memory differently. If the dog had seemed at all dangerous, I highly doubt my father would have encouraged me to go swing right where the dog was lying. I don't think I was at all nervous around dogs. In fact, my whole childhood all I wanted was a dog of my own. Probably I ran over to the dog and startled it. I've seen my younger daughter make plenty of sweet-natured dogs and cats nervous enough to bark or hiss at her. When I wrote about this incident in high school, I probably needed to make my father somehow responsible for the incident, because I was in the middle of trying to understand my relationship with him. Now, as a father myself, I see the dynamics of this kind of situation in a different light, and so if I were to rewrite this story, I am certain that I would re-create many of the details differently to reflect my current understanding.

One set of events, one set of facts, but multiple truths.

Tobias Wolff, who has written memoirs of his childhood and his experiences in Vietnam, explains why it is impossible to capture your past exactly as it occurred.

> We tend to think of memory as a camera, or a tape recorder, where the past can be filed intact and called up at will. But memory is none of these things. Memory is a storyteller, and like all storytellers it imposes form on the raw mass of experience. It creates shape and meaning by emphasizing some things and leaving others out. It finds connections between events, suggests cause and effect, makes each of us the central figure in an epic journey toward darkness or light. (2001)

We need to approach memoir with the understanding and with the acceptance that we can't remember everything that has happened to us exactly as it happened. Most of us can't even remember in great detail what happened to us the day before. At the beginning of his memoir *The Adderall Diaries*, Stephen Elliott (2009) offers the disclaimer: "Only a fool mistakes memory for fact." And it's true. Recount a past experience a hundred times, and no two tellings will be exactly the same. In fact, each retelling, though growing progressively more distant from the event, has the potential to reveal more layered truths as new experiences daily deepen our understandings of the world and of who we are.

How Do You Help Students Overcome the "I Don't Remember" Syndrome?

When students say they don't remember anything—and they will say this—I've learned to acknowledge the feeling rather than try to prove to them that they remember lots of things. I mean, of course they remember lots of things, but it's far better if they come to this on their own. And they probably don't mean what they're saying literally, anyhow. They're usually just feeling that it will be impossible to spin any past experience into a full ten pages.

"It really is hard to remember things that happened a while ago," I say. "It's hard for me too."

This makes them feel a little better, but not much. There's still the problem of how they're going to write a ten-page memoir.

"I remember things that happened," they might say, "but I don't remember any of the details."

One strategy that is often effective in this situation is to ask students to imagine how things might have happened. If a student only remembers getting into a big argument with her mother but does not remember exactly what it was about, or what was said, I ask her what kinds of things she and her mother usually argued about and to describe to me how these arguments would typically go. I tell her that she will be inventing the dialogue, and I remind her that this is what all memoir writers do because it is impossible to re-create a scene exactly as it happened.

"But what if I really can't remember at all?" she might ask.

Here I would invite students to discuss what it is about themselves, their relationships, or their lives they are trying to convey with the particular scene or story and to re-create the details in a way that will most clearly and powerfully convey these larger truths. If my student tells me that she wants to show how her mother is much too overprotective, I encourage her to re-create details and dialogue that will show this idea without stating it explicitly.

For some students, this is enough. Given permission to re-create the details from past experiences in a way that *feels* truthful, they are able and ready to go. Still, it is always helpful to look back at published models and discuss what we think the writer remembered, and what we think the writer invented. For example, take the title story in Adam Bagdasarian's *First French Kiss*. The author writes about going to Maggie Mann's party in sixth grade and making out with her. Here he re-creates their first conversation.

> "Hi," she said.
>
> "Hi."
>
> For a moment that was all I was able to say. Just the sight of her took my breath away.
>
> "Have you tried the onion dip?" she asked.
>
> "Not yet. Is it good?"

She nodded. "I made it."

I intended to say, "Well, if you made it, I know I'll like it," but it came out "Oh."

Just then, Joanne waved to Maggie across the room, made a face, and mouthed something.

"I think Joanne wants to talk to me," Maggie said.

"Okay," I said. Then, remembering that this was my night and that I could do no wrong, I added, "Will you save the first slow dance for me?" (2002, 3)

It doesn't take much prompting for my students to see that the author probably took a vague memory of an awkward first conversation and imagined the way it might have gone. What grownup can remember what food was served at a party in sixth grade? Onion dip? Give me a break. But it's a nice detail. And it works to make a barely remembered interaction feel real. Of course it didn't happen exactly like this, but in the author's memory, this is what it felt like to be a sixth-grade boy at the party of the sixth-grade girl who liked him.

The importance of helping students distinguish between fact and truth cannot be overemphasized. Each year students report that their inability to remember the details of past experiences is one of the biggest roadblocks they face as they grapple with what to write about. And each year, as students come to understand that memoir is largely an act of artistic invention, that the inadequacy of memory is not so much a limitation as it is an opportunity to shape their stories as they see fit, they begin to feel liberated and are finally able to move forward in their work of looking back.

Where Does Memoir Cross the Boundary into Fiction?

In 2003, Doubleday Books published *A Million Little Pieces*, James Frey's "memoir" of alcohol and drug addiction and his painful rehabilitation. Two years later, it became Oprah Winfrey's Book of the Month selection, which propelled it to an extended run atop the New York Times bestseller list.

But in 2006, everything started to unravel. Writers for The Smoking Gun, an investigative website, published an article called "A Million Little Lies" describing a series of fabrications they had uncovered in Frey's account. Appearing on *Larry King Live*, Frey responded to the charges.

> My side is I wrote a memoir . . . A memoir literally means my story,
> a memoir is a subjective retelling of events . . . The book is 432 pages
> long. The total page count of disputed events is 18, which is less than
> five percent of the total book. You know, that falls comfortably within
> the realm of what's appropriate for a memoir . . . I've acknowledged
> that there were embellishments in the book, that I've changed things,
> that in certain cases things were toned up, in certain cases things were
> toned down, that names were changed, that identifying characteristics
> were changed . . . I still stand by the fact that it's my story. It's a truthful
> retelling of the story. (Frey 2006)

Frey's claim that his story is truthful, even if it is not entirely factually accurate, seems to suggest that his work falls within the acceptable boundaries of memoir. But the nature of Frey's embellishments, along with the fact that he admits, later in the interview, to first shopping his manuscript around as a work of fiction, calls his claim into question. For example, Frey writes that he spent three months in an Ohio jail, when in fact he was there for only a few hours. He describes hitting a cop with his car, getting into a fight with the police, and being charged with felony, DUI, and possession of narcotics, none of which actually happened.

When Larry King asks, "Did you, frankly, embellish a criminal past?" Frey's claims to truth become less convincing:

> I mean, Larry, I've acknowledged I've changed things . . . But the
> primary focus of the book is not crime. The primary focus of the book
> is drug addiction and alcoholism, and that's why the book takes place in
> a treatment center. You know, it's a book about getting better, you know.
> It's a book about dealing with problems. It's a book about redemption
> and pain and family . . . In the memoir genre, the writer generally
> takes liberties. You know, you take liberties with time because you're
> compressing time a lot. You take liberties with events and sequence of
> events. The important aspect of a memoir is to get at the essential truth
> of it. (Frey 2006)

There is a difference, I would argue, between re-creating something you don't remember as you think it might have happened and blatantly lying about your past. Frey's claim that his fabrications don't alter the fundamental truth of his memoir is undercut by the fact that he presents himself as someone he was not. It is one thing to take liberties with your past in an effort to reach a higher truth. But it is something else entirely when you include deliberate fabrications meant to enhance the drama of the narrative and to paint a more compelling protagonist.

"Think of it this way," I tell my students. "Suppose you're writing about the first day of middle school, and you want to show how scary it was. You remember that the older students all seemed so big and that you didn't know anyone and that you were afraid the teachers would be mean, but you can't remember anything bad that actually happened."

I see my students nodding, because this describes what the first day of middle school was like for many of them.

"Does it seem likely that some of the older kids were talking in the hallways about how small you new sixth graders looked?"

"That happened," one of my students says.

"So even if you don't remember exactly how it went, you could create a scene in which a group of eighth graders is talking or laughing at how small you are to show how scary it felt on that first day."

I see that my students are with me, so I continue.

"Now suppose you really want to emphasize that the first day was terrifying, and you want to make the story more dramatic for your readers. Would it be okay to create a scene that didn't really happen, like having a group of eighth graders surround you at your locker and threaten to beat you up after school?"

My students laugh and shake their heads.

"Why not?" I say. "Don't you think that would help show how scary the first day was?"

"You can't just make things up," one of my students says.

"But you're making up all the dialogue," I persist. "What's the difference?"

"You're not making it up," the student says. "It's based on what happened."

"Yeah, it's still basically true," another student adds. "But if you just make up something completely like getting beaten up, it's fiction, not memoir."

And there you have it.

A Final Paradox

I keep several binders of all the memoir writing I have done over the years. From time to time, I go back and read something I have written long ago, and I am always grateful to be able to relive these stories from my past. Reading about my Bar Mitzvah lessons with old Mr. Friedman, I am taken back to that little room behind the sanctuary where we would study together. Flipping through my account of living in New Orleans in the early '90s, I smile as I am reminded of a life that seems almost foreign to me now twenty years later.

The funny thing is that even though writing these memoirs has enabled me to preserve my past, what I ended up writing has become more real to me than what actually happened. Annie Dillard captures this paradox perfectly.

> If you prize your memories as they are, by all means avoid—eschew—
> writing a memoir. Because it is a certain way to lose them. You can't
> put together a memoir without cannibalizing your own life for parts.
> The work battens on your memories. And it replaces them. It's a
> matter of writing's vividness for the writer. If you spend a couple
> of days writing a tricky paragraph, and if you spend a week or two
> laying out a scene or describing an event, you've spent more time
> writing about it than you did living it . . . After you've written, you
> can no longer remember anything but the writing . . . Memory is
> insubstantial. Things keep replacing it. Your batch of snapshots will
> both fix and ruin your memory of your travels, or your childhood, or
> your children's childhood. You can't remember anything from your
> trip except this wretched collection of snapshots. (1987, 156–157)

Without disputing this observation—because it is so wonderfully insightful and true—I would just reiterate the following point. We don't write memoir to preserve the past exactly as it happened. We write memoir to reach a higher truth about our lives and about who we are. Yes, when we write memoir, we cannibalize our lives for parts. There's no avoiding that. The trick is knowing what parts to keep and what parts to leave out.

That's what the next chapter is about.

CHAPTER 5

Story and Understory

My student Vincent is writing a memoir about going to Coney
Island with his mom when he was five. He recounts what
he was doing at home before he left. He describes the trip
on the subway. He includes lots of detail about the different rides and attractions.
He talks about eating Nathan's hot dogs. He really does an admirable job giving
me a play-by-play account of what happened on that day.

"What makes this story significant?" I ask him.

He says that it just stands out in his memory.

"Why does it stand out?" I ask.

He shrugs and says it was a fun day.

"It sounds fun." I wait to see if he will say anything more. Then I ask, "What
else makes it stand out?"

He tells me that when they were leaving Coney Island, he accidentally stepped
on a woman's foot and she started yelling at him and then his mother started
yelling at the woman and he just really remembers that.

"Tell me a little bit more about what happened," I prompt, and as he speaks it starts to become clear that beneath the story of Vincent's trip to Coney Island lurks a deeper story about his relationship with his mother. I nudge him in this direction by asking him to tell me more about his mom and their relationship, and he starts telling me about how his mom works all the time so he doesn't see her much, and how she is really strict, but can be fun and crazy too.

"I'm starting to understand why that day at Coney Island stands out in your memory," I say.

Vincent nods. "We hardly ever do stuff like that together."

"Remember the work we've been doing with story and understory," I say. "When you go back to work on your memoir, look for places where you can bring out these ideas we've been talking about."

I don't remember when I first heard the term *understory*, but I've used it with abandon ever since. It signifies that there is something lurking beneath the story's surface, a deeper significance, and it is our job as writers to bring it forth. Over and over again, I push my students to think about what their stories are really about, why they matter, what they reveal about themselves and their relationships and their lives. For Vincent, the story of his day at Coney Island was a vehicle to explore his relationship with his mother, and by the time he turned in his final draft, he had written a memoir that was about much more than just the events it recounted. Yes, he tinkered with his past in choosing what parts of the day to re-create and what parts to leave out, but in doing so he took an unremarkable experience and uncovered something deep and significant lurking within.

One of my favorite published models for teaching the concept of story and understory is a vignette called "The Bird Hunter" from Adam Bagdasarian's memoir *First French Kiss*. I read this story with my class and ask for a volunteer to retell the plot, which basically involves the writer's obsessive desire, at age twelve, to shoot and kill a bird and how the experience of actually doing so ends up being extremely traumatic for him.

"So that's what happens in the story," I say, after the retelling is finished. "But what's it really about on a deeper level?"

Hands shoot up.

"It's about his first experience with death."

"It's about how killing and death are not as glamorous as they seem in the movies or on TV."

< 57 >

"It's about wanting to feel powerful."

My students get that there is more to the story than the events that transpire. They understand that the author has chosen to share this particular story because there are deeper ideas about himself and the world that he wants to convey.

"Let's look at the very end of the story," I say.

> I tried to shrug off the murder and not let my friends see how I really felt. I'd never really trusted them, for the same reason that bird couldn't trust me; and I walked home alone that day, feeling as ghastly as the first man after he'd taken a bite of the wrong fruit in the Garden of Eden. (2002, 88)

Not all of my students are familiar with the reference, so I ask for a volunteer to share the Bible story. And then the light bulbs begin to click on.

"It's about loss of innocence," someone volunteers. "He didn't truly understand death until this experience."

Someone else jumps in. "Maybe killing the bird is like killing his innocence."

We go back into the story and examine the way the writer brings out these big ideas by the details he chooses to include and the details he chooses to leave out. It is a hugely important lesson that my students will need to grasp in order to weave story and understory together effectively in their memoirs.

How Do Memoir Writers Decide Which Details to Include and Which Details to Leave Out?

"Imagine you were planning to write a memoir about a family vacation to Paris," I tell my students, "and you've made a list of things you remember about the trip." I hand out a sheet of paper with a list of memories.

FAMILY VACATION TO PARIS

Your family argues about where to go.

Your airplane is delayed three hours.

You have an intense fear of flying and are convinced the plane is going to crash.

You are excited because every seat on the plane has its own TV.

< 58 >

While you are flying, you daydream about what it would be like to live in the clouds.

One piece of your luggage is missing when you land.

You and your brother get your own room in the hotel.

Your father wants to see all the tourist attractions and drags you around the city.

You go to a restaurant and accidentally order snails because the menu is in French.

You are constipated for the entire trip.

You and your brother order a pornographic movie on pay-per-view.

You stand in line for two hours at the Eiffel Tower.

You sit on a park bench and make up stories about the lives of the people you observe.

You and your brother discover the mini-bar in your hotel room.

You get lost wandering around the Louvre.

You learn how to swear in French.

You learn to eat foods you never thought you would like.

Your mother gets sick, and you have to spend a whole day in a hospital waiting room.

You find out that both your parents used to smoke.

The fire alarm goes off in the middle of the night at your hotel.

You meet a girl your age who is staying at the same hotel, and you exchange addresses.

You are sad when it is time to leave.

"How do you know which details to include and which details to leave out?" I ask.

What I want my students to understand is that the point of memoir is not to re-create every single thing that happened. The point of memoir is to illuminate what made a particular experience significant and to include only those details that help bring out this understory. So I have my students practice.

"Turn over the page," I tell them.

Here is what it says on the back:

What do you emphasize?

What do you leave out?

Understory #1

I get through life by never taking anything too seriously.

Understory #2

Growing up is about taking risks.

Understory #3

Things in life that seem horrible sometimes turn out better than expected.

Understory #4

My relationship with my parents is complicated.

The understory of the memoir—that is, what the memoir is really about—will dictate which details to emphasize and which to leave out. So I ask my students to put the number 1 next to any detail they would include if understory #1 were driving their narrative. They go back to the sheet and choose details that bring out the understory of never taking life too seriously. Daydreaming about living in the clouds, for example, or learning to swear in French. Then I have them repeat this exercise with a second understory. They notice that certain details will work for more than one understory. They might also observe that any detail could potentially fit any understory if manipulated in a certain way. But it becomes clear to them that they have the power to steer their story in different directions and bring out different truths based on what they choose to emphasize and what they choose to leave out.

The writer Annie Dillard, in discussing her process while working on her memoir *An American Childhood*, puts it as follows: "The writer of any work, and particularly any nonfiction work, must decide two crucial points: what to put in and what to leave out" (1987, 143). She goes on to explain how she makes these decisions in her own work, and begins her explanation by asking the question:

"Well, what is the book about?" And it is her answer to this question that dictates her decisions.

> I leave out many things that were important to my life, but of no
> concern for the present book, like the summer I spent in Wyoming
> when I was fifteen. I keep the action in Pittsburgh; I see no reason to
> drag everybody off to Wyoming just because I want to tell them about
> my summer vacation. You have to take pains in a memoir not to hang
> on the reader's arm, like a drunk, and say, "And then I did this and it was
> so interesting." (1987, 154)

Russell Baker sets out to write the memoir of his childhood during the Great Depression and realizes after submitting a four-hundred-and-fifty-page manuscript that he has written something that even he cannot get through without nodding off. As a journalist, he had done his research, conducted his interviews, double-checked his facts, and produced an extremely long piece of journalism, rather than a compelling story. What he comes to realize is that he never had a clear sense of what the memoir was really about.

> I had lunch with Tom [my editor] and said that I knew what was
> wrong with the book and that I would rewrite the whole thing. I said
> it was a book about a boy and his mother. It was about the tension
> between a child and his mother, and everything had to hinge on that.
> And Tom said he thought that was right—that I had made a grievous
> mistake in trying to write a book about myself in which I didn't
> appear. (1987, 33)

Does Every Memoir Need to Have an Understory?

Every memoir—every good memoir—needs to be about more than just the events it recounts. Even a memoir that is about something with obvious significance needs to go beyond simply retelling what happened. Think back to *The Rice Bowl*. The events themselves are incredibly compelling, but it is the writer's ability to fashion those events into a deeper story about human resilience and the bonds of family that makes the memoir so moving and powerful.

< 61 >

When I discuss the need for understory in memoir, it is really the same thing as discussing the need for themes in all literature. Mark Twain's *The Adventures of Huckleberry Finn* would never have become a classic had it only been an adventure story about a boy and a runaway slave rafting down the Mississippi River. What makes the book so great—beyond Twain's mastery of language—is how brilliantly the author uses the story to comment on questions of freedom, racial prejudice, the collision of law and conscience, and other issues society was grappling with at the time. Similarly, Melville's *Moby Dick* is about more than a hunt for a whale, Shakespeare's *Hamlet* is about more than a prince trying to avenge his father's death, and Frost's "The Road Not Taken" is about more than a hiker in the woods trying to decide which path to take. In each of these cases, plot and theme are inextricably wound together to open a window into the world of the characters and to illuminate the human condition.

A memoir can have multiple understories, just as a novel can have multiple themes. Even student memoirs, only ten pages long, often delve into several different ideas, though in these memoirs there is usually a main understory—a main theme—the author is exploring. This main understory can be apparent to readers on page one, or emerge only at the end. It can be a single driving idea, or several different ideas that intertwine. It can be something the writer has figured out before starting to write, or something the writer only uncovers after working through several drafts. Whatever the case, the writer's goal is to convey to the reader that the memoir is about more than just the events it describes, and the understory is the vehicle through which this occurs.

How Do Memoir Writers Bring Out Understory Most Effectively?

There are no hard and fast rules here, but there are lessons we can take away from reading great memoirs. First and foremost, writers need to be able to articulate why they are writing a particular story and what makes it significant. It was only when Vincent identified that his story about Coney Island had significance for him because it was really about his relationship with his mother that he was able to revise his narrative in a way that allowed this understory to emerge.

Also, students need to remember that they are not obligated to retell everything that happened. They should emphasize details that reveal something about

< 62 >

them and help convey the ideas they want to bring out, leaving out details that are not necessary and that do not develop the understory.

It is possible to find an understory in almost any topic, but the most effective understory is one that reveals something deep and meaningful about the writer and his or her world. My student Emma wrote a draft of her memoir about skiing. I asked her about her understory, and she was able to point out that a lot of her stories involved her close friend. At the same time, she realized that her memoir did not really open a window into this friendship, and that it revealed almost nothing about who she was.

"I didn't want to write a memoir about friendship," she admitted. "I just wrote about skiing because I have lots of memories."

Rather than trying to manufacture an understory from her experiences, Emma decided to change topics and write about something that she knew would reveal more about herself and her world, namely her parents' divorce and how it had affected her. While I generally discourage students from switching topics each time they hit a roadblock, I knew Emma well enough to recognize that this new topic would yield much more fruit for her. And indeed, once she began to write, her memoir became less a chronicling of events and more a deeply personal story about love, family, loyalty, and redemption. Focusing mostly on her strained relationship with her father, here is how she decided to end her memoir to bring out the understory she was trying to convey.

> *Dad and I are sitting at a baseball game . . . the game has gone into extra innings.*
>
> *"If we lose this I will be so pissed. We need today . . . But it's very likely that we will lose, because . . . well, Dad, we suck."*
>
> *"Emma, something I've learned in my life as a Mets fan is that sometimes you just need to believe in your team. Granted, every year we suck, and that never surprises me, but sometimes we do amazing things."*
>
> *The inning has turned over, now it's the 11th inning and the score is tied at five.*
>
> *"But that's really not okay. We have all the players that we need to make us a good team but we can't win."*
>
> *My dad smirks at me. "We won last night."*
>
> *"Yeah, but we lost to the Reds two out of three games when we were there."*
>
> *"We believe in comebacks, don't we?"*

. . . The top of the inning is over, and we're now up to bat. Henry Blanco, the catcher is up to bat. The pitch is delivered and contact is made. We stand up to watch the ball soar through the air. It goes right past us, to the back wall, and soars over the orange line. It's a home run.

Dad turns to me. "That's how we do it!" I'm screaming and cheering. A smile is painted across my face. Sometimes even those who consistently disappoint you can do things that fill you with joy.

Emma weaves her understory directly into the fabric of the story she is telling, so that plot and theme become inextricably bound together. Going to the Mets game with her father was an important piece of her story, as it stands out as one of the few positive experiences they have had. But what makes the scene indispensable is that in her feelings for the Mets, Emma has uncovered a perfect analogy to illuminate her feelings for her father, so the final scene is about more than what the words themselves convey. We are left with the feeling of a story well told, largely because the ending so artfully ties together the big ideas she has been exploring.

This technique of finding a symbol in the story that can stand for something deeper is a particularly effective way to bring out the understory. We see it in *The Rice Bowl*, where the rice sticking together in the bowl represents the way the family has managed to hold together. We see it in my story of getting bit by a dog where the distorted shapes of the shadows represent my altered perspective of my father. And we see it in my student Rihana's memoir *Prom Shoes*, a fifty-one-page magnum opus that stands out as the longest memoir I have ever received from an eighth-grade student.

The writing throughout Rihana's memoir is phenomenal, and each of the seven stories is driven by a strong understory. The title story comes last. After moving us through elementary school antics, the social stresses of middle school, the intense pressures of getting into an elite high school, and her parents' struggles with each other and with the American Dream, she takes us to the days before prom where she and her friend are shopping for shoes. The story itself fits perfectly into the fabric of her memoir, as it brings her narrative up to the near present. More important, though, it introduces a perfect metaphor to encapsulate all the powerful ideas about peer pressure, image, identity and independence that she has brought to bear.

The right shoe. I had to find the right shoe for me. Elena's model shoes would not work for me. I had to find my own shoe. It wouldn't look anything like Elena's shoe, but it would make me look like a star. My shoes would shine a spotlight on me on prom day and wherever else I wore them. I had to find my own shoes. The right shoes for me. I didn't know what they would look like but I would find them.

Here again we have a story and an understory that are inextricably tied together, and an ending that leaves readers thinking about the deep ideas the writer has raised during the course of the narrative.

Prom Shoes and *The Rice Bowl* have something else in common. The symbols that help bring forth the understories emerge not just at the end of the memoirs, but are the actual titles of the memoirs themselves. Coming up with a title that carries this kind of symbolic meaning—think *To Kill a Mockingbird* or *The Catcher in the Rye*—is yet another way to bring the story beneath the story to light.

*   *   *

I pass out a copy of Vincent's memoir, cleverly entitled *Bumper Cars*. "I want to look at a memoir one of my past students wrote," I say. "On the surface it's about a four-year-old boy spending a day at Coney Island with his mother, but of course it's about more than that. Let's look at the details he includes to bring out his understory."

Bumper Cars

The first time I went to Coney Island I was in my cute annoying stage, that area of childhood when you look like a big cabbage patch doll. I was four years old. It was Saturday and out of the blue my mother said we were going to Coney Island. Being my four-year-old self, I said, "Mommy I want to watch Thunder Cats." It was not that I didn't want to spend time with my mother, it was just that Thunder Cats was the most important thing in the world to me at that time.

My mother, clearly annoyed, said, "Vincent, I took off work so we could go together. You have to come with me."

"Don't wanna, Mommy. Thunder Cats Hooooo," I bellowed.

My mother, being the resourceful woman she was, appealed to the one weakness which could possibly make me do anything, a bumper car ride. It was my Achilles Heel, the one thing that could pull me away from Thunder Cats.

"Well," she said, "I'll have to ride the bumper cars all by myself. And the cotton candy will be too much for me."

"Bumpy cars," I said, suddenly interested. "Bumpy cars big, but still don't wanna."

When I said that, my mom smirked as if she knew she had me even though I didn't realize it. She knew me better than I knew myself. "Well, then, you want to go shopping with me?"

Death. Well, at least to a four-year-old it is, and my mother knew it. Going shopping with my mother would sap all the fun out of me. My four-year-old brain knew that Macy's meant death by boredom, so my choice was clear: death or some place called Coney Island.

As I got ready, I washed up and Mommy gave me a new Alligator shirt to wear. I had to give it to my mother, she sure could dress a four-year-old. After I was ready, Mommy said, "Bookie, would you like some candy to take?"

"What kind?" I said, hoping for chocolate.

"Mister Goodbar," she said.

At that moment, even Thunder Cats couldn't have made me happier. Chocolate and bumpy cars, it was too good to be true.

The ride to Coney Island was bumpy and noisy although I was the one making most of the noise. "We there yet? We there yet?"

"Nooo," she said, barely keeping her anger in check. I could tell because her voice was approaching that shrill yell, like the Furies of Greek myth. My four-year-old "don't get Mommy mad protection system" kicked into high gear.

"Thank you, Mommy," I said, hoping to cool the furnace.

"Do you know," my mom said after a short silence, "there are hot dogs at Coney Island."

"What kind?"

"Nathan's, but even better than the ones we eat at home."

I was in the clear. She wouldn't have mentioned hot dogs if I wasn't. We got off the train and Mommy told me we were almost there in a happy-go-lucky tone of voice. And then, with a smile on her face, she grabbed my hand and we began to run down the slanted platform onto the street, not caring what anyone thought of us. In my four-year-old mind, Mommy was faster than Wonder Woman and we were going a million miles an hour.

To me my mother always seemed super human. She was a figure who in many ways mystified me. At the time, we were living with my great grandmother and, aside from weekends, I only saw my mother when I was waking up and going to sleep. There was so much I didn't know about her and she was constantly surprising me. Taking off like a mad woman down the subway platform was a perfect example.

My mind soon shifted to thoughts of Nathan's hot dogs and bumpy cars and then to the other possible treasures awaiting my arrival. Questions raced through my mind. Did they have any games there? And if so, what kind? Would I be tall enough to ride their bumpy cars? My mind eased as we entered a gaming Mecca. A noisy, dirty, raggedy Mecca, but a Mecca just the same. I happily sloshed through the trash-littered ground. I ran my mommy ragged, turning her more times than a merry-go-round. I pointed and oooh'ed and ahhh'ed at everything. Then Mommy took me by the hand and pointed to something. At first I couldn't make it out, but then I saw it, shining like a hot dog TAJ MAHAL. The Nathan's hot dog stand. My tongue watered.

"You wanna hot dog, Vincent?" my mommy asked.

"Hot dogs!" I yelled. My wish was granted. Walking to the stand, images of mustard covered franks and golden brown buns danced across my mind. I came out of my daydream as we stood in front of the vendor. I THINK I heard him say, "What would you have, Miss?" in an accent I now recognize as Pakistani, but I can't be sure. To me he seemed to be a mile high.

"What kind of hot dog you want Vincent?"

"Ketchup and mustard," I said, my teeth ready to tear into the bun. As I looked up I could see Mommy eyeing the man like a hawk. She always inspected food that was cooked for her or for me. Even at four I knew that Mommy would make a fuss if food wasn't prepared to her liking. If a cheeseburger wasn't cooked enough, if French fries weren't hot enough, you could bet the farm that it would be sent back with a few choice words. I prayed to God that my hotdogs would pass mustard.

The hotdogs appeared and I grabbed them, but my impending bliss was halted. It was my mom.

"What do you say?" she asked me.

What did she want from me? I had said thank you, hadn't I? I guess not. How could I forget Mommy's Golden Rule?

"Thank you, you're the best Mommy in the whole world," I blurted out.

"You're welcome," she said. "Next time remember faster."

That was my mother. Always a stickler when it came to manners. From living with my great grandmother, I could see it was something that had been passed down for generations. It was funny to imagine Mommy being told the same thing when she was younger.

With the hot dogs now resting in my stomach's sweet eternity, it was time for the bumper cars. My mother thought differently.

"Don't you want to go on the roller coaster?" she asked me.

"What about the bumpy cars?" I asked, wondering why she had changed my plans.

"We'll go on the bumper cars, but wouldn't it be fun to go on the Astro Ride first?" She said the name of the ride so dramatically that I was reluctantly swayed to try it. I had no idea what I was getting myself into.

In line I started to get nervous. "Mommy, I have to go to the bathroom now."

"Too late, Vincent, we're almost there."

My overactive imagination kicked into full gear. I began thinking about episodes of Mission Impossible where a seemingly nice lady had tricked Jim to go on an airplane with almost no fuel. Was Mommy trying to trick me? Why was she making me go on the ride now? When a menacing looking man buckled me into my seat with a double lock bar, I was positive something was wrong. I thought about all the times I had made Mommy angry. The broken mayonnaise jar, the lost glove, and of course the fried chicken incident. She had never forgiven me for stealing that chicken out of the oven.

The car began to climb the ramp. It seemed like it was taking forever for it to reach the top. Then, for a split second, it teetered on the top, and I could see all of Coney Island. The people looked like ants. Then we fell, or should I say plummeted. We kept gaining speed, and I felt lunch reaching for my throat.

"Having fun?" yelled Mommy, her arms swinging wildly.

We hit the first loop. I could feel my cheeks flapping in the wind.

Then the first twist. Just like Mission Impossible.

So I had uncovered my mom's fiendish plot, but she'd have to get up pretty early in the morning to get rid of me so easily. I was a Mission Impossible fanatic and knew all the tricks. We twisted again, but I wasn't gone yet. A few more twists and turns and it was over. Dazed, I stepped out of the car.

"Wheee," said Mommy, "wasn't that fun?"

It seemed like she had replicated, and five mommies mingled in my vision.

"Whew," they said, "what a ride!"

I was still alive after the ride so my Mission Impossible honed survival skills were laid to rest. I was now pretty sure Mommy forgave me for the chicken incident and wasn't trying to get rid of me after all. With that problem solved, my full attention was now on bumper cars. "Now we go to bumpy cars, Mommy?" I asked.

"Okay, Vincent," she said, "we can go now."

As we walked to the car place my eyes began to droop. I yawned. Oh, man, I thought. If Mommy saw me getting tired we'd be on the first train back to Grandma's, which would mean no bumper cars, and I couldn't have that. Luckily Mommy didn't seem to notice my yawn, which was strange because she usually eyed me like a hawk when walking. We arrived at the bumper car place. As we walked onto the line, images of crashing cars and bloodied bodies filled my mind. "RUMMMMMM," I said, talking in my deepest and bestest car-sound voice.

"We're here," Mommy said, and she was right. My fun had just begun.

I stepped onto a big ruler. The clown's bright red nose was the highest my head reached. "Just made it," said the guy at the ruler. "Go right ahead." The line was huge. A bunch of kids were before me. I mumbled to myself, "Stupid line, all those big kids. Can't they go to another line?" I was careful to say all this under my breath so my mother wouldn't hear me whine. It was a known fact that Mommy hated when I whined, and if she ever heard me it would guarantee a loud and long sermon on patience and I REALLY didn't have the patience for that.

Finally it was our turn. Mommy wanted to drive our car, but I grabbed her hand. "Let me drive."

"Alright, are you sure?" She seemed doubtful I could pull it off.

We jumped in and Mommy immediately put on her seatbelt. "You too," she said, and then helped me when I became helplessly entangled. The music began and the cars came to life. Sparks flew from the lifelines connecting the cars to the ceiling. I had just begun to push the gas when I was violently jolted from behind. I swung the wheel and faced my attacker, a lanky man with freckles dotting his cheeks. My mom was laughing and this only made me angrier. How could she laugh at something like this? She should have been helping me ram him harder than he had rammed me. The war was on. I stomped on the gas pedal,

< 69 >

maneuvering past the other cars as I honed in on my intended victim. Mom was on my side now cheering me on and strengthening my resolve. For the next three minutes we waged a private war. It seemed as though there were no other cars except ours, engaged in a shifting game of hunter and prey. Then, as suddenly as it had started, it stopped.

As we exited I felt a supreme satisfaction in knowing I had won. I probably wouldn't have even needed my mother, but it was nice to have her there. It was becoming dark all around me, but I didn't even notice. "It's time to go," my mother said, and I didn't really mind. I had done what I had come to do.

The train station was already in view when I was jarred from my thoughts by a shrill voice.

"Oww, damn, knocking me down boy, quit knocking me down. Watch where you're going."

I looked around and saw a heavy-set black lady in her twenties glaring down at me angrily, but before I could respond in any way, I heard my mom's extra-authoritative voice.

"Don't you talk to my son like that. This is my son, I raised him, not you. I'll discipline him."

"He should watch where he's going," she said in a voice subdued by my mother's fury. "Just make him watch where he's going."

"Don't worry about him," she said. "If he stepped on your foot you tell ME not him. Just go about your business. He's sorry." My mom grabbed my hand and we stormed away. I could tell she was angry.

"You need to watch where you're going," she said, glaring down at me. "Stop knocking into people and pay attention.

"But I didn't feel her foot," I pleaded. "I didn't hit her."

"Yes you did Vincent, don't lie to me boy," my mother screamed as I started to become teary eyed.

"But I-I-"

"Come on, boy," my mother growled. "Let's go."

As we left Coney Island my mind reviewed everything that had happened that day. Bumpy cars, roller rides, hot dogs, crazy ladies with foot problems, and Mommy still yelling—wow what a day, I thought.

"HURRY UP!" my mother cried. "Let's go home."

On the train ride home, I fell asleep, my cotton candy plastered cheeks resting lightly on my mother's shoulder, her hands resting lightly on mine.

I finish reading, look up, and face my class. "So," I say. "Who can tell us what this memoir is really about?"

CHAPTER 6

The Sea and the Mountain

O n the board, I draw a picture of a mountain overlooking the sea. A lone figure stands perched atop the mountain's summit and another swims among the waves below. The picture is terrible, downright comical in its badness, but my students get the idea.

"What do you think this picture means," I ask, "and what does it have to do with writing memoir?"

Over the years I've gotten a wide range of responses to this question. One student suggested that it might represent the highs and lows of a person's life. Another said that maybe the person in the ocean drowned and the person on the mountain is his ghost looking back at his life. A third person thought it might have something to do with being able to look at your life from different perspectives.

We get into a discussion about the different ways the two people view the ocean, how one can see the water stretching endlessly, while the other can see floating seaweed and swelling waves in sharp focus. The person on the mountain sees the big picture from afar; the person in the water is assaulted by his immediate surroundings.

When we write memoir, we want to move back and forth between the sea and mountain. That is, we want to zero in on the sights and smells and sounds and feelings of past moments in such detail that our readers can fully experience these moments for themselves. At the same time, we want to zoom out from these moments and reflect on how and where they fit into the grand scheme of who we are and the lives we've lived.

Consider the following passage from Tobias Wolff's memoir *This Boy's Life*. Notice the way in which he skillfully moves from the sea to the mountain, by putting us in the middle of the action, but also reflecting on the scene that is unfolding.

> I slept badly that night. I always did when my mother went out, which wasn't often these days. She came back late. I listened to her walk up the stairs and down the hall to our room. The door opened and closed. She stood just inside for a moment, then crossed the room and sat down on her bed. She was crying softly. "Mom?" I said. When she didn't answer I got up and went over to her. "What's wrong, Mom?" She looked at me, tried to say something, shook her head. I sat beside her and put my arms around her. She was gasping as if someone held her underwater.
>
> I rocked her and murmured to her. I was practiced at this and happy doing it, not because she was unhappy but because she needed me, and to be needed made me feel capable. Soothing her soothed me. (1989, 55)

We experience what it was like for the young Tobias Wolff to have to switch roles with his mother, to be the one to take care of her. But we also get the more mature insights of the adult writer, who reflects on why he enjoyed and embraced taking on this role.

Or consider this passage from a story called "The Fight" in Adam Bagdasarian's *First French Kiss*.

> Soon I could not distinguish one punch from another, and my ears burned, and the noises around me seemed to be coming from a

< 73 >

hollow tube . . . And then one, by one, or two by two, the lights went out in my mind, and Mike's legs were around my stomach and I couldn't breathe.

"Give?" he said.

I shook my head.

He squeezed harder. "Give?"

Why not? The last light in my mind said. All I'm giving him is the fight. So I gave: I gave him the fight, the love notes, the phone calls, the envy, the adulation, and the arrogant hull of who I had been.

For a moment I felt very light, almost weightless. (2002, 71)

This is the concluding passage of a story in which the author lets us experience all the anxious moments leading up to a fight, then makes us ringside spectators when the punches begin to fly. At the same time, even as the lights are going out in his mind, his mountaintop persona is sharing a revelation. This, he realizes, is the moment when the image of himself he has created finally shatters. His final line combines the perspective of the sea with the perspective of the mountain —the feeling of losing consciousness with the knowledge that life actually becomes easier when you no longer have to carry the burden of extreme popularity.

Many students struggle to write effectively from either of these perspectives. Often they tell their stories in a way that neither captures the drama of their experiences nor offers insights to explain how these experiences fit into their larger life stories. Therefore, before we push students to integrate these perspectives, it is important to show them how to write effectively from each one and to provide models for them to study and imitate.

How to Help Students Write from the Perspective of the Sea

You've probably heard the writing commandment, "Show, don't tell." This is the key to writing from the perspective of the sea. Instead of telling about an incident that occurred in the past, the writer re-creates the incident as a scene.

The components that go into re-creating a scene effectively are dialogue, descriptive action, access to the character's thoughts and feelings, and sensory detail. All of these things work to bring the reader into the middle of what is unfolding. Different scenes might rely more or less heavily on these different components, but generally speaking, some combination of these things helps bring past moments to life.

Lucy's memoir is largely about her complicated relationship with her mother. Rather than just explaining the awkwardness and discomfort she often feels in her mother's presence, she re-creates specific memories so that readers can more fully experience these feelings for themselves. In this excerpt, Lucy wakes up to "the smell of uncertainty and liquor" and finds her mother passed out on the couch bed in the living room.

I peek cautiously into the living room. My mother is covered by a thin white knit blanket. She is sprawled out, stretching from one end of the bed to the other, a tuft of hair where her head should be. She looks almost inhuman, or deranged. I go through my normal morning routine, only silently, crossing the living room only when absolutely necessary. I get dressed in the bathroom, as always. I put on black pants, a long-sleeved black shirt and a grey vest. Waking her up would be embarrassing for the both of us. What do you say in a situation like that?

After running through the living room a few times, I feel it's safe to say that my mother is fairly knocked out. Once more walking through I stop and stare at my mother's figure under the blanket, and my heart stops. It is too big, too lumpy, and has too many limbs. There is too much hair in that one tuft to come from only one head. In the same couch bed that had held my eight year old sleepovers, my mother had had a sleepover of her own. I am fairly sure there are two women under that raggedy old blanket.

At this point, I panic. I run through the house. I have to get out of here. I don't want to see any more. I don't want to know any more.

I am running by the couch bed as fast and as silently as possible, the floorboards creaking under my feet. My mother stirs. I freeze. I bite my thumbnail and just beg she does not wake up.

Can you picture it? Can you feel what Lucy must have been feeling at that moment? The awful realization that her mother is not alone under that blanket? The desperation of trying to get out of the house undetected? We're emotionally invested because Lucy has brought us into the scene with her. Notice all the ways in which she has accomplished this. She opens by dropping us into the middle of the action. She writes in the present tense to make what is happening feel even more immediate. She is specific in her description and lets us know what she is thinking and feeling in the moment. She builds suspense.

Here is how the scene ends.

> *She wakes up.*
>
> *Very few things stay with me.*
>
> *"Oh. You're dressed," she says at one point. She hands me lunch money in a robe. She crosses her arms, almost hugging herself and gives the covered woman an odd, sad look. I leave the house as soon as possible. And we never talk about it again.*
>
> *Except once.*
>
> *"That woman this morning, that was . . . Sue Ann. She's from the company."*
>
> *"Oh."*

That's it. The scene ends there. There are no reflections on the significance of this episode, no deep insights woven into the narrative, no indications of how her understanding of the event has changed over time. These elements do exist when the scene is read in the context of the rest of the memoir, but here Lucy's intention is to write from the perspective of the sea, to bring us fully into a moment and allow us to experience what she experienced.

Teddy draws us into his scene by having us follow a bouncing Ping Pong ball down the basement steps. Once there, it is not unfolding action or dialogue that we experience, but rather the feverish workings of his imagination. He does not tell us what it's like to be afraid; he shows us.

> *I heard the ball bounce down the steps into the basement, heard each tap echo throughout the damp room beneath Dustin's house. I placed my foot on the first step into the basement. It creaked loudly. I looked around at the water heater and radiator and the many unused tools that so many wealthy families have strewn about their homes. I quickly hurried down the steps . . . "Click." I heard the light switch flicked off. "Creak," the door closed. There was complete and utter darkness, the kind of darkness one can't even imagine, one can only experience or remember. I stood stone still where I was, like a gargoyle, my vocal chords knotted up in my throat impairing my speech and hampering my breathing. Reluctantly I drew in a shaky breath.*

I was alone save for the menacing hum of the radiator.

Not knowing what I could not see, my imaginative mind made up horrors left and right to terrorize my helpless brain. Something with long serrated claws and with gleaming red eyes was in the room with me. Its unmoving, unchanging pupils watched me from a point in the room, calculating the moment to pounce and kill, jump and cut, strike and stab.

It would take one long, razor sharp, paper thin claw and draw it across my belly, slicing it open with a slow agonizing swipe, and my intestines would spill out onto the floor. Its long cold clammy fingers placed on the back of my neck as three-inch long incisors punctured my jugular and dark red blood spewed across the ceiling. No one would know, no one would hear, the unknown that the darkness is would swallow everything up.

I waited to feel my stomach tearing open, to feel the warm blood gush down my pants and well up in my shoes. Only it wasn't blood, but piss. I vaguely noticed that I was pissing in my pants, but still I anticipated a strike from the darkness.

But no strike came, I did not feel the searing burn of torn flesh or hear the sickening "splotch" of corded gut spilling onto the floor, my bowels leaking a foul odor into the air about me. I was alone save for my thoughts and the low hum of the radiator.

How to Help Students Write from the Perspective of the Mountain

I want my students to understand that time and age and distance alter our perspectives on who we are and the meaning and significance of our experiences. To make this concept more concrete, I give them some prompts to think and write about.

Think of a time in your lives when something happened that seemed like a huge deal at the time, but now doesn't seem so important when you look back on it.

Think of a time in your lives when something happened that didn't seem like such a big deal at the time, but now seems more important when you look back on it.

Think of something you understand about yourselves now that you didn't realize or recognize when you were younger.

Or, I might just give them the following prompt and have them fill in the blanks in as many different ways as they can think of.

< 7 7 >

I used to think _____, **but now I think/know** _____.

It is important for students to understand that one of the reasons why memoir writers need time and distance from the events they are writing about is because when we are in the middle of things, we often are not able to grasp their full significance or how they fit into the larger story of our lives and of who we are. When we write from the mountain, we are asking ourselves: _What do I understand now about this story that I did not fully grasp when I was living through it?_

Sometimes we can express these more mature understandings explicitly. Luna's memoir about her experiences in an extremely nontraditional elementary school is entitled _Me, Lady Philosophy?_ in reference to the tall brass statue that greeted her when she arrived at school each morning. In the memoir's final section, Luna positions herself firmly on the mountain and reflects on her years at the school and what she has come to understand now, when she looks back on it all.

> _My years at Abraham Lincoln School were filled with discipline, sobriety and comedy now and then. I now realize that, although it wasn't the best education I could have gotten, it exposed me to things I did not appreciate at the time. Then, I thought that the Met was boring to go to every Friday, but now I realize how lucky I was to be so near it. I also thought that meditation was only a time to speak sign language to my friends, but lately I wonder if there might be something to it. I believed that Sanskrit was just more homework to do and philosophy a thing for old people. Now I want to remember those teachings, but not the teachers. I wonder if my experience at Abraham Lincoln School would have been more positive if the principles stayed the same, but if there was more room to create myself. I've realized many things since leaving Abraham Lincoln School but mainly that you can't shape a sculpture by pounding on bronze, and you can't force a sassy, sarcastic girl into the mold of Lady Philosophy._

Luna needs to have time and distance to understand the impact her experiences had on her. From the mountain, she is able to see that things that seemed one way when she was experiencing them seem different when fit into the larger story of her life. What makes this last section so memorable, though, is the final line, which cleverly invokes the title and brings the memoir's understory to full fruition.

< 78 >

Sometimes, the writing from the mountain is not so apparent and does not include sentence starters like, "I now realize . . ." or "What I have come to understand . . ." or any number of other variations that explicitly signal that the writer is about to engage in the act of reflection. More often, mountaintop writing is just observations or insights woven into the story that the character was probably not consciously aware of at the time or would not have been able to articulate. We see this throughout Luna's memoir, starting on the first page where she describes arriving at school every morning and passing the statue of Lady Philosophy: "She was everything we were expected to aspire to. This tall, brass woman, roaming in a beautiful garden with hands outstretched, represented wisdom, serenity, and the true Self. She was everything the school wanted to show us about self-realization and inner beauty."

That's a smart eighth grader talking, not a kid still in elementary school.

Writing from the mountain is really a natural extension of many things I have discussed in earlier chapters. When we cull our memories and decide what's worth writing about, we are positioning ourselves on the mountain. When we uncover our understories and reflect on the larger truths we are trying to convey, we are doing so from the perspective of our present selves. When we think about the lives we have lived and how all the pieces fit together, we are, in effect, standing on the mountain and looking out over the sea.

Putting It All Together

Skilled memoir writers move seamlessly between sea and mountain somewhat unconsciously. In putting their lives on paper, they are naturally re-creating experiences as powerfully as possible and examining those experiences from their present perspectives. The point is not to have a perfect balance. Nor is it to be able to identify every passage as being either from the sea or the mountain. Rather, it is to be conscious of the ways in which we can bring readers fully into the lives we have lived and convey the truths about ourselves and the experiences we have uncovered.

Here Anika is writing about a visit with her dying uncle. Notice how there is no clear division between writing from the sea and writing from the mountain, but how we nevertheless experience the scene both from the perspective of a seven-year-old child and from the perspective of an older, more reflective writer.

A few days before Stasiu's death, I remember entering the hospital room in which he lay. A breeze flew in through the window, and the sun's rays set a color on the pale white walls. He lay in the third bed from the entrance and was the only patient in room 306. I walked up to his bedside and greeted him cheerfully. He turned to look beyond my 7-year-old body to see my grandfather and grandmother smiling. His eyes turned away from the two and locked with mine. An unusual feeling came over me, for I knew that this hospital bed, with bed sheets emitting the faint smell of Tylenol and Aspirin, was the last thing to witness his battle for his last breath. He was aware of the arrival of death, and yet he did not answer when family members parted with him after a few minutes of conversation telling Stasiu that he must surely visit them after his recovery.

"You've grown!"

I only smiled, revealing my toothless front jaw.

"I could swear you grow an inch every time I see you." He picked up my hand and squeezed it among his ten scrawny fingers.

"What do the doctors say?" my grandfather asked from behind me.

"What should they say?"

"Do they think you're doing better?"

"Ahhh . . ." he sighed, and looked out the window to view the light green leaves of the cherry trees. "Screw all the doctors, what do they know? Remember Witek, grandmother would give us some nasty tasting liquid and we would get all better, just like that." He snapped his fingers. "No hospital, no doctors, nothing." He waved his hands in front of him with little strength.

My grandmother stepped up and grasped me by the shoulders. "We better get going. Gabrysia is making dinner, and we really do not want to be late." She tapped him on the arm and smiled.

A feeling of loneliness came over me. All people ever did was enter and greet with Stasiu, to part with him after five minutes of conversation. He was no longer considered a normal person, for the only place he was able to be seen was in bed, with many needles placed under his skin and plastic tubes rising from his veins. He let go of my hand, seeming to me as if he was letting me reenter my life. For the time spent in that room was to fade away and only leave me with the satisfaction of having visited an ill family member. For when he was to pass away, I would be able to tell people I cared, I visited him, once, I kissed him on the cheek and headed for the door.

< 80 >

"Want an orange?"

I turned back to see him raising the fruit.

"I won't eat it anyway. I don't know why they give it to me."

It seemed to me, if I was to take that orange, it would leave him with a satisfaction of showing compassion for the day. I reached out and took it from him. "Thanks," and I left room 306.

Go back and look at all of the things Anika is doing in this excerpt. Notice how the writing flows naturally between dialogue, descriptive action, and her private ruminations. Notice the details that help us visualize the scene. Notice the way she weaves in her deepening understandings of what she is experiencing.

Let's revisit Vincent's memoir about his trip to Coney Island. Throughout his story he moves seamlessly between the four-year-old character, who is experiencing the events, and the eighth-grade writer, who is uncovering deeper meaning in what transpires.

"What kind of hot dog you want Vincent?"

"Ketchup and mustard," I said, my teeth ready to tear into the bun. As I looked up I could see Mommy eyeing the man like a hawk. She always inspected food that was cooked for her or for me. Even at four I knew that Mommy would make a fuss if food wasn't prepared to her liking. If a cheeseburger wasn't cooked enough, if French fries weren't hot enough, you could bet the farm that it would be sent back with a few choice words. I prayed to God that my hotdogs would pass mustard.

The hotdogs appeared and I grabbed them, but my impending bliss was halted. It was my mom.

"What do you say?" she asked me.

What did she want from me? I had said thank you, hadn't I? I guess not. How could I forget Mommy's Golden Rule?

"Thank you, you're the best Mommy in the whole world," I blurted out.

"You're welcome," she said. "Next time remember faster."

That was my mother. Always a stickler when it came to manners. From living with my great grandmother, I could see it was something that had been passed down for generations. It was funny to imagine Mommy being told the same thing when she was younger.

Your students should look at their own memoirs through this lens of the sea and the mountain. Are there places where they can bring their readers more fully into memories they are sharing? Are there places where their present-day voices can offer the deeper observations and insights that come with time and distance and age?

CHAPTER 7

Beginnings, Endings, and Titles

There once was a famous writer who said, "There are three tough parts to writing a novel, a story, a poem, or any sort of writing; the beginning, the middle and the end." I wholeheartedly agree . . . As I'm sure you've noticed, I'm not very good at beginnings. As I'm sure you will notice I'm not very talented with middles either. But on endings, however, I hope I am right in my assessment that I can at least keep the story in your mind for a little while. To summarize, I think I'm good at endings. Just watch. This section ends here.

—*Only One: A Memoir About a Boy, a School, and a President* (Brian's eighth-grade memoir)

Have you ever had the experience of knowing what you want to write about but not knowing how to start? It can be almost paralyzing, right? Either you stare at a blank page or you keep writing beginnings and then crossing them out because they're terrible. This chapter is about how to help students get over all that and write great beginnings to their memoirs. It's also about how to help them write great endings and come up with great titles.

< 83 >

How to Write a Great Lead

Plato called the beginning "the most important part of any work." Lao Tsu spoke of how "a journey of a thousand miles must begin with a single step." Horace believed that "he has half the deed done who has made a beginning." And in her poem "Elegy in Joy," Muriel Rukeyser (2013) writes:

> Nourish beginnings, let us nourish beginnings.
> Not all things are blest, but the
> seeds of all things are blest.
> The blessing is in the seed.

When I work with my students on writing the leads to their memoirs, we look together at a bunch of different great beginnings and name what it is each writer is doing. We create a list of these different techniques, and then we try a few of them out.

Most great leads do more than one thing. For example, a memoir that begins with a poem might also fall into the category of a memoir that opens by introducing the theme. A memoir that introduces the narrator might also be directly addressing the reader. Here I've classified leads into categories based on one thing each does well. What they all have in common, though, is the power to hook a reader.

DIRECTLY ADDRESSING THE READER

This is the most direct way for a writer to establish an immediate connection with his or her readers. Here David uses the word *you* several times in the opening sentences to make it sound as if he is speaking directly to his audience.

> *First of all let me tell you right off the bat that this is going to be a very boring memoir. If you are looking for a very well written dramatic memoir read* This Boy's Life, *and if you prefer a sappy drama go watch* 7th Heaven. *But if by some blind twist of fate you happen to be an English teacher who assigns children memoirs, read on at your own risk.*

< 84 >

STARTING WITH THE REPETITION OF "I REMEMBER"

The rhythmic repetition of "I remember" establishes the primacy of memory as storyteller and creates the effect of a drop of water, rippling out into ever-widening circles. Here Samarra draws us deeper and deeper into her early memories of living with her grandparents.

> *I remember the blue linoleum counter and paper plates as the TV growled in the background. I remember the cluttered bedroom filled with religious speakers saying the good of God, the hazy purple bedroom and the hard mattress that I still sleep on. I remember when my grandfather used to yell words of hate and anger at my mother, grandmother's hands over my ears. I remember when I saw my grandparents finally leave the house and when I thought that it would get oh so much better. Boy was I confused.*

STARTING WITH DIALOGUE

There's something undeniably appealing about eavesdropping on a conversation. Here Amelia re-creates an exchange with the school guidance counselor that pulls us immediately into her life and piques our curiosity to know more.

> *"Have you ever tried to hurt yourself?"*
> *"No."*
> *"Have you ever tried to hurt someone else?"*
> *"No."*
> *"Do you plan on hurting yourself?"*
> *"No."*
> *"Have you ever thought about hurting yourself?"*
> *I kept eye contact, but did not respond as we sat in silence. Then she repeated her question.*
> *"Have you ever thought about hurting yourself?"*
> *"I guess."*
> *"You guess, or you have?"*
> *"I have."*

< 85 >

STARTING WITH ACTION

Similar to starting with dialogue, starting with action pulls readers into the story right away and lets them experience the drama of the moment. Here Sally uses vivid detail to bring us right onto the stage with her as she begins to perform.

> The darkness lifts. The lights flash on. Red! Green! Yellow! The audience quickly silences. You can hear a pin drop, "Ting, ting, ting ahh, ling ing, ng . . ." The pianist begins to play. The music is soft, yet in a way, mysterious. The stage is empty and huge in my eyes. As I start to move to the music, I can feel my stomach growl. I slowly start to sweat. I feel the humidity under my outfit. I feel as if little bugs are crawling up my skin. As if they going up my legs and arms . . .

STARTING BY INTRODUCING THE SETTING

Introducing the setting allows readers to visualize the world where the story begins immediately. Here Marcus gives us a specific location, but also uses sensory detail to describe what it feels like to be in this place.

> On 26th Street between First and Second Avenues, you might hear an echo of a net being caressed by the sweetest of jump shots or the heartbeat-like pace of a ball being dribbled. You feel the rhythm in the heels of your feet from every corner of the neighborhood. Everyone who lives there knows these sensations. They are caused by Marcus playing his heart out.

STARTING BY INTRODUCING THE THEME

Introducing the theme does not necessarily mean announcing it explicitly; it means showing one or more big ideas you will be exploring in your work. Here Roxanne does not explicitly state what her memoir is about, but uses specific examples and a whole lot of voice to highlight her theme of racial identity.

> Just to make it clear I can do the "Lean Wit It Rock Wit It." It's a new dance that came out from Dem Franchise Boys that anyone who is black or Latino is required to know. I can do it but I find it hard to do in front of people because at school I've been labeled white. Someone like Snoop Dogg can put on a shirt and tie and a knitted sweater and still be called black. I can try everything to prove that who I am is actually black but I'd still look like a joke. Ever since kindergarten when I started noticing that I was different in terms of color and race compared to others,

I've been changing and molding myself to the cultures and people around me. Even today I have two personalities: I can act one way in my neighborhood where I'm cutting out syllables and saying things like, "I'ma deck that niggah in his fucking face, he thinks I'm playing with him." I've been acting white for so long in school that if I came out saying something like that people would be telling me to stop trying to act black.

STARTING BY INTRODUCING THE NARRATOR

If writing memoir is about revealing who you are, then why not introduce yourself right off the bat? It's a chance to show how interesting or funny or friendly or screwed up you are—to make an immediate connection with your readers and invite them to hang out with you for a little while. Here Daniella grabs us by the lapels and begins rambling about herself in a way that just makes us smile.

HI! I'M DANIELLA! There's really no reason for the first sentence to be in caps, except I like the fact that I'm yelling in your head. It gives me some sort of weird power over you . . . I guess you should know a little about me before you decide to give up this memoir as a lost cause . . . I love basketball and I don't suck. I don't like cliques, people who break promises, pointless things, losing, prejudice, bad singers, bad actors, pepsi, lentils, and bananas. I like sports, winning, chocolate, Italian food, puppies, speaking my mind, rhyming poems, being right, watching TV, guys, Usher, Ellen DeGeneres, reading good books, and listening to a song I like until I know all the words . . .

STARTING BY INTRODUCING A CENTRAL CHARACTER

If you don't want to throw yourself into the spotlight right away, you can begin by introducing another character that will figure prominently in your memoir in some way. Here Lucy chooses to introduce her mother in a way that hints at the drama to come and makes us eager to know more.

My mother is not fat. Nor is she skinny.
When I am little, she gives me half of her pizza, for she can't finish it. She repeatedly skips meals, but I think nothing of this when I am young.
I'm unsure of how old I am when I first hear the sounds. Probably in the sixth grade, just learning how to hide, and the art of being awkward. I hear sink water running in the bathroom. Mom is washing up. This is normal enough, but tonight

it sounds different. There is a sick sound under the water that makes me freeze to a point of silence. Under the cold faucet sounds are the sounds of retching, of pressure on my mom's throat. I think she may be sick, and so I don't ask.

STARTING WITH YOUR NAME

Discussing your name is a specific way of introducing yourself. Names carry a lot of meaning for many people and play into how they perceive themselves. My first young adult novel begins with the protagonist discussing his name, and I have used this technique in some of my own autobiographical writing.

I was born without a name. I was supposed to be Max, but when my grandfather found out, he begged my parents to reconsider. He was a Holocaust refugee, and Max, he said, sounded too German. So, in the end, my birth certificate said Baby Boy Wizner, and it was not until several days had passed before my parents settled on a name. Jonathan. It would turn out to be a name that almost nobody who knew me would ever use.

STARTING WITH A PROVOCATIVE OR INTRIGUING QUESTION

A question that makes readers think or piques their interest is another great way to draw them into your piece. Here Gigi asks something that might seem obvious on the surface, but then follows up her original question with other questions and a statement that challenge our initial thinking.

What is a home? Is it a ceiling and four walls? Is it a warm bed at night and a cool breeze in summer? Is it a physical place at all? Over my short 14 years of life, I have learned that a house is not a home.

STARTING WITH A SHOCKING OR DRAMATIC STATEMENT

This is a surefire way to grab the attention of your readers. It's like being a boxer who just climbs into the ring and immediately throws a knockout blow. Stephen Elliott begins his memoir, *The Adderall Diaries*, with the following sentence:

My father may have killed a man. (2009, 3)

Impossible not to continue reading after that. If nothing quite so dramatic has happened in your life, consider other ways you might shock your readers and

< 88 >

grab their attention. Here Henry lulls us into a sense of tranquility and then hits us with something entirely unexpected.

Lake George is a great place to bike in, especially if you go on the bike path near the water. The crashing of the waves against the rocks becomes a rhythm, the chirping of the birds becomes a chorus, and the sound of running over the used condoms thrown along the path becomes lyrics.

STARTING AT THE END

There is something intriguing about knowing how a story will end and watching events play out toward this conclusion. Here Anika opens with the striking image of viewing her uncle's corpse, and then the memoir jumps back to tell the story of his death.

I walked in through the polished wooden doorway, to step into a room with a corpse in front of the altar. The dim light highlighted the dust particles floating about in front of the stained glass, representing The Last Supper. The aqua blue eyes of Jesus were focused on the room filled with weeping women and men dressed in black tailored suits. Held by the hand, I was taken up to the casket and lifted to gaze at my uncle.

✣   ✣   ✣

I tell my students to write at least three possible beginnings for their memoirs, using (or combining) different techniques for each. Volunteers share their beginnings with the class, and we vote each time on which beginning we like most and why. When we move back into writing time, many students take one of their beginnings and run with it. Others continue to experiment with different leads until they hit on one they love.

How to Write a Great Ending

I run an Alfred Hitchcock elective at my school in which I show *The Birds*. Students love the movie and sit transfixed as the main human characters stagger into their car after surviving the latest brutal onslaught by the island's birds. As they start to drive off, the movie suddenly ends.

"It's over?" my students ask incredulously, and then they proceed to tear apart what they consider a completely unsatisfying ending. Their anger stems from the fact that so much is left unanswered. Will the people get away? What is the answer to the mystery of the birds' behavior? Is this going to turn into an all-out global war between humans and birds? Who would win?

Not all of my students hate the ending. A few say that all the unanswered questions enhance the suspense. The fact that we will never know what causes the birds to act the way they do is much more unsettling than having a neatly packaged answer.

The way you end a memoir, or any work for that matter, is critical because it is the final impression you are leaving your readers with and will often shape their whole understanding of the story. In his classic book *What a Writer Needs*, Ralph Fletcher devotes an entire chapter to endings. In his words, "The ending may well be the most important part of a piece of writing. It is the ending, after all, that will resonate in the ear of the reader when the piece of writing has been finished. If the ending fails, the work fails in its entirety" (1992, 92).

I ask my students, as they are working on their endings, what it is that they want their readers to be thinking or feeling when they put the memoir down. And their answers to that question will drive the decisions they make about how and where to end the stories they are telling.

Beyond identifying what you want your readers to think and feel is the question of technique, and here the process for writing a great ending is similar to the process for writing a great beginning: identify endings you love, name what it is that makes each ending so good, and experiment with these techniques in your own writing. Following are some student examples.

COMING FULL CIRCLE

There is something very satisfying about this technique. Perhaps it is because a circle feels complete, unlike a line, which can stretch on forever. Here Abby starts her memoir on her porch steps, then flashes back to tell the story of her relationship with her father, and then returns to where she started at the very end.

Beginning

Today is warm and sunny. The light is reflecting off the trees. It reminds me of a Matisse painting . . . I walk over to the porch steps and sit down. Then I notice something as I look at my cement walkway and suddenly a memory jolts my head. I think of my father whom I haven't seen since I was four. The one square block of cement, as I recall it, was the last place I saw him . . .

Ending

And so I sit on my front steps and the memories of my father flash right before my eyes, and I look out at my front yard, at the flowers that in time will bloom and I look at the last place I saw my father . . . I walk over to my front door and I twist the big brass doorknob and I look back one last time at what remains. A square block of cement that my father waited on, once upon a time.

EPILOGUE

An epilogue is a great way to tie up loose ends and provide information that might not fit in the main body of your story. Here Zeke brings us forward in time to tell us how things changed for him in the years that followed the events of his memoir.

Two years went by and the same things kept happening over and over again. But my teachers weren't right. It wasn't my immaturity. It was something else, something that was going on inside my brain. There was an imbalance—an imbalance of specific chemicals in my brain. It took a doctor to figure out that my hyperactivity, my impulsiveness, my inability to focus and concentrate was due to the fact that I had ADHD.

I was diagnosed in second grade, and since then I have changed…I don't get into trouble for being impulsive, I do well in school, and people can't tell I'm taking any medicine unless they see me after it wears off.

I can't imagine what it would be like if I didn't take medicine.

Oh wait, I can. That would be like kindergarten through second grade—those glory days of great stories.

Been there. Done that.

PHILOSOPHICAL

A philosophical ending does not tie everything up neatly. Instead, it leaves us to think about big questions or ideas about life and human nature that the work has introduced. Here Gigi challenges us to rethink our notions of embracing familiarity or venturing into uncharted waters.

Almost all of the people I know would never think of moving, they are so deeply rooted in the place they were born and raised. To them, moving is stupid; unnecessary. Change is scary, unnatural. The untraveled road, the room with no light to turn on. Why take the risk of the unfamiliar? Why would you travel to the darkness, when you are so enveloped in the light?

JUMP TO THE PRESENT

Jumping from the past to the present gives readers a fuller picture of how the events of the narrative continue to impact the writer in his or her present life. Here Jeremy jumps forward in time and switches to the present tense to give a sense of where he is now.

I am an eighth grader. The times of my past are in the past, though I may look back on them . . . The spaceships I imagined and built of Legos sit in the corner, awaiting a call from their commanders to start up and fly out and battle. The books that are veterans of my hands ask for another reading, the ones not yet perused beg for me to pick them up. Drawings and scraps and notes all cry for the examination of my eyes, before they find themselves in a place of honor. Abandoned works for the night, they all seem to desire a revisiting. Then I realize one last thing, before I flip the switch on the light.

There's still an empty page in the typewriter.

RIDING OFF INTO THE SUNSET

Usually this is a poignant moment, the stranger who is galloping off from the town he has just saved, or the couple that has finally found love and is embarking on a new life together. Here Trevor subverts those romantic notions as he bids a harsh farewell to one era of his life and prepares to embark on the next phase of his journey.

At the sound of the bell, the last day of school was over, and with it we never had to go back to P.S. 116 ever again. Some had tears in their eyes, while others laughed and enjoyed themselves. Outside school, people gave and received hugs.
Except for me of course.
Everyone gave a final goodbye and a firm handshake to all of his buddies.
Except for me of course.

Some were even going to go to a party at a friend's house to say a final farewell. Not me of course.

Everyone turned to look at our elementary school, saying they were going to miss it dearly.

Except for me of course. I was happy to move on.

At the last moment, I turned for one final look, then silently turned my back to everything—the kids, the school, the memories, and walked heartlessly away.

FINAL METAPHOR

Incorporating a final metaphor is a great way to bring out your understory at the end of your piece. Here Marcus uses a basketball shot to represent his drive to succeed in life.

My eyes become moist as I finally make my way to the court. This is the only day I don't welcome the rain. As I shoot a few jump shots, I remember all the ballers who could have had a chance but ultimately fell victim to some sort of dilemma. I can't help but think about the chances of me falling to a challenge like all the others before me. Why should I be spared when others weren't? I set up to shoot not thinking of anything but the shot. I begin to see all the places the ball can take me. I jump straight up into the air, the rain hitting my face, trying to keep me down. Still, I continue upward and when I reach the peak of my jump I release the ball with a graceful flowing forward momentum. As I float back toward earth I see the ball glide through the sky hurling all the raindrops out of its way until finally it hits nothing and drops perfectly through the net.

ILLUMINATING THE TITLE

Sometimes a writer does not reveal the full meaning or significance of the title until the very end of the piece. Brian wrote a fifty-page memoir, entitled "Only One." It is a hilarious and comprehensive journey through his years in middle school. You forget about the title, until the end of his epilogue.

Throughout history and throughout the future thousands of kids will pass through the Salk School of Science and thousands of kids will have stories to tell. Of all these, I am but one, of all the classes I am a member of only one. And of all my classmates, some of whom I will never meet and some of whom I have shared three years, some of whom belong to the class of 2004, all of whom I feel a connection to, I have only one of the many stories, experiences, and school lives. Of all the students in the Salk School of Science, and in my class, I am only one.

How to Come Up with a Great Title

Figuring out your title can happen any time during the writing process, but for me it almost always happens near the end. For example, as I work on this chapter right now, I have no idea what the title of this book will be, though I have a list of possibilities, none of which I love. I hope in the end I come up with something that offers a clear sense of what the book will be about, but in a catchy and original way. (Did I pull it off?)

When I work with students, we analyze titles of books and movies to figure out what makes some titles better than others. We come up with a list of great titles that ranges from *To Kill a Mockingbird* to *South Park: Bigger, Longer, and Uncut*.

"A good title shouldn't be too obvious," one student says. "It has to make you think."

Another student disagrees. "Not always. I think *Star Wars* is a good title, and that doesn't make you think."

Some titles are funny. Others are dramatic or arouse the reader's curiosity or just sound cool. Whatever their taste, students should remember that the title is one of the biggest advertisements they have for their work, so it's important that they come up with something that will catch a reader's attention.

I often become paralyzed trying to come up with a perfect title. One way I overcome this is by challenging myself to come up with five titles in five minutes (or ten titles in ten minutes). I have used this activity each year with my students, and they have really enjoyed it. Most of the titles, admittedly, are not great, but occasionally something pops out that is rather wonderful.

In general, I encourage my students to keep a running list of possible titles, to experiment with titles that vary widely from one another, and to model their titles on titles they love.

Of course it is impossible fully to appreciate or evaluate a title without reading the work, but here are some student memoir titles that strike me as wonderful, even standing on their own.

Funny Titles
Camp Stories That Don't End in Obscene Games
I Shoulda, Coulda, Woulda . . . But I Didn't

Dramatic Titles
He Never Meant to Hurt Me
The Monsters in My Closet

One-Word Titles
Moonshine
Veritas
Anthrax

Riffs on Other Titles
The Good, The Bad, and My Family
Fast Times at 55 North Elliot
Strange Encounters of the Third Kind

Titles That Begin with the Word **Confessions**
Confessions of a Twinkie
Confessions of a Wheelchair
Confessions of a Tortured Teen

Titles That Juxtapose Seemingly Unrelated Words
Elephants & Airplanes
Worms and Whiskey

Titles That Have Symbolic Meaning
Bumper Cars
The Elephant Army
She's Leaving Home

A Final Note

I focus exclusively on beginnings, endings, and titles in this chapter, but the process of identifying authors' techniques and experimenting with those techniques in their own writing is something students can do throughout their memoirs. Look back at Chapter 3 for other examples.

In addition, even though all the writing models in this chapter came from memoirs, many of the ideas I discuss and the strategies I present are applicable to other genres of writing as well. In other words, if I ever write a book about teaching students to craft short stories, don't be surprised if you see a chapter that looks an awful lot like this one.

CHAPTER 8

Assessment and Evaluation

Read the following passage about memoir, and answer the questions that follow:

Excerpt from "How to Write a Memoir" by William Zinsser

Most people embarking on a memoir are paralyzed by the size of the task. What to put in? What to leave out? Where to start? Where to stop? How to shape the story? The past looms over them in a thousand fragments, defying them to impose on it some kind of order. Because of that anxiety, many memoirs linger for years half written, or never get written at all.

What can be done?

You must make a series of reducing decisions . . .

Don't rummage around in your past—or your family's past—to find episodes that you think are "important" enough to be worthy of including in your memoir. Look for small self-contained incidents that are still vivid in your memory. If you still remember them it's because they contain a universal truth that your readers will recognize from their own life. (2006)

1. According to William Zinsser, what challenge paralyzes most people who set out to write memoirs?

   a. Finding enough time to write

   b. Being overwhelmed by the size of the task

   c. Remembering important events

   d. Being unwilling to make reducing decisions

2. What advice does Zinsser offer?

   a. Don't rummage around in your past

   b. Look for small self-contained incidents that are still vivid in your memory

   c. Piece together the fragments of your life into some kind of order

   d. Try to relate your life to the lives of your readers

3. Why did the author write this piece?

   a. To share details of his own life

   b. To describe the challenges in writing a memoir

   c. To offer advice on how to write a memoir

   d. To correct the misconceptions people have about how to write a memoir

There is something very neat and clean about judging our students' learning using multiple-choice, standardized tests. Answers are either right or wrong, students (and teachers) from different schools can be easily compared, and individual learning can be neatly tracked. Beyond that, analysis of reading test results can yield valuable data about students' strengths and weaknesses and insights into the learning of different racial, gender, and socioeconomic groups within our classrooms.

But overreliance on these tests does more harm than good. As our school system becomes more and more driven by test results, the kind of memoir work I have been describing in this book starts to be supplanted by more and more test preparation. In her book *Writing a Life*, Katherine Bomer includes a whole chapter on how students can use memoir writing to excel on the writing sections of standardized tests. She does an admirable job showing how teachers can use the rich work she has been describing as part of their test preparation, but the fact that she has to link the two is in itself a little depressing, something she herself notes as she begins the chapter:

> To move from talking about revising memoir as a way to gain
> perspective on one's life to talking about preparing for school tests
> seems like a move from the sacred to the profane. It's sad but true that
> our students compose their lives within a school system that continually

wants to measure whether they are good enough to continue progressing through those lives. (2005, 175)

And in their book *New Directions in Teaching Memoir*, Dan Kirby and Dawn Latta Kirby make the case against standardized testing as follows:

> We have never seen a multiple-choice exam created by anyone that can adequately inform us about our students' writing abilities. Even the state mandated tests that actually require students to write are still often isolated, artificial evaluations . . . and their existence still consumes precious instructional time spent, not in meaningful activities for learning but in focusing on teaching the test in order to raise the all-mighty scores of the school and district . . . Such tests are inappropriate and virtually meaningless instruments for informing anyone about students' abilities to write well. (2007, 141)

Assessing and evaluating the learning that takes place during the memoir unit is not as neat and easy as scoring standardized tests, but it is significantly more valuable. Rather than measuring students' ability to perform well on a single test administered over a period of one or two days, the assessment and evaluation in a well-developed memoir unit provides a far more comprehensive and meaningful picture of our students' abilities to showcase the kind of thinking and learning we should be trying to nurture in our schools. Here are some examples.

Are students able to uncover patterns and themes in their lives?
Students brainstorm memories and then find different ways to group them together. They link together different events and uncover thematic connections in seemingly unrelated episodes from their lives.

Are students able to reflect deeply on who they are and how they have changed over time?
"Who Am I?" is one of the big questions that drives the whole memoir unit. Discussions, reflections, and the memoir itself reveal how deeply the students delve into this question.

Are students able to examine past events from multiple perspectives?

Students re-create past events through the eyes of their younger selves and reflect on how their perspectives have changed and deepened over time. They also bring other characters to life and re-create the ways in which those characters might have experienced these memories.

Are students able to identify and analyze author's craft and incorporate techniques they see into their own writing?
Students read with the eyes of writers, identifying examples of writing that jump out at them and naming what the writers are doing to make their words come alive. Throughout the unit, they have multiple opportunities to imitate and practice the techniques they are learning.

Are students able to critique their own writing and the writing of their peers effectively?
Students learn strategies to give each other feedback. As they become more comfortable recognizing and naming strengths and weaknesses in the work of their peers, they become more attuned to turning the same critical lens on the writing they are doing themselves.

Are students able to revise and edit effectively?
Students have several weeks to revise and edit first drafts. They learn and practice strategies to reenvision their work, grapple with how best to incorporate teacher and peer feedback, and strive to make their work as clear and clean and compelling as possible. They have the opportunity, in other words, to experience the whole writing process and do the work that all writers do.

Are students able to articulate their own writing processes?
Students become more highly attuned to their own processes as writers. Do they work better in notebooks or on a computer? In school or at home? Do they work off an idea and see where it takes them or plan in detail before they start writing? Coming to know themselves better as writers has huge implications for increasing the chances that they will be successful.

Are students able to meet deadlines and manage time effectively?
This is not about rushing through questions to finish a timed test. It is about learning to chunk a long-term project into manageable pieces, learning to make

productive use of unstructured time, and learning to go that extra mile when necessary to ensure that neither deadlines nor standards of excellence fall by the wayside.

What Is the Difference Between Assessment and Evaluation?

In a thesaurus, these words are listed as synonyms, and in dictionaries, one is often used to define the other. In teaching, however, I have always drawn a distinction. For me, assessment is about gathering information about what students are and are not able to do and using this information to inform my instruction. Evaluation is also about gathering information about what students are and are not able to do (at least as reflected in the work they have turned in), but instead of using this information to inform my instruction, I use it to assign a grade.

At the same time, while I link evaluation to grading, these grades then become another form of assessment as we move on through the year. By examining a student's grades on different projects and tasks, I am able to make better plans for working with that student as we move forward.

How and When I Assess My Students During the Memoir Unit

There are many ways and many opportunities to track and assess student progress during the memoir unit. Much of this assessment is informal—observing students as I walk around the classroom, checking in briefly with them as they work, noting what they have to say during class discussions. Where I gather most of my information, though, is through written reflections the students submit, one-on-one writing conferences that I conduct with each student, and completed first drafts that I collect about two-thirds of the way through the unit.

REFLECTIONS

It is important to have students reflect on the work they're doing throughout the unit. Dan Kirby and Dawn Latta Kirby (2007) provide a comprehensive menu of reflection formats to be used before, during, and after writing. These include various planning documents, status reports, and self-assessments. One of their planning suggestions is a "Memoir Blueprint," which prompts the students to think like architects who need a blueprint of a building to check out its design and supervise its construction. The authors provide students with a blueprint planning sheet that students fill out and use as a guide as they begin to work.

This kind of handout can be tremendously useful to students and can help teachers assess where students are and what kind of support they need. In general, I prefer my students to reflect in a more open-ended format, having them grapple with their ideas in paragraphs rather than filling out a form. I usually require a one- to two-page reflection as they're getting started, two more while they are composing their memoirs, and a final one at the end of the process. This translates to a reflection every two weeks or so, because if I require more than that, students become sick of reflecting and I get overwhelmed with how much work I am collecting. I don't give the students assigned topics, but we spend time discussing what kinds of questions or issues seem worth thinking deeply about.

Early on, the students' reflections often revolve around the question of what's worth writing about and why.

> For my memoir I have thought about many things to write about. First I was thinking about writing about my love for basketball . . . I have written about this many times before so I thought for this project I would write about something else in my life. So another topic for my memoir is my vacation to Disneyworld when I got lost . . . I might write about this moment because it was something big that happened, and it shows the love that I have for my family and the love they have for me. The last thing that I might want to write about is the most serious thing I could write about, how my father got caught and went to prison. I was only seven, and I didn't understand back then, but now I realize why he is where he is. This is the saddest thing in my life. I can't experience what a son is supposed to with a dad, because he made a poor judgment at a young age. He was 16 when I was born, and he went to prison at 23. He only saw seven years of my life so he is gonna miss my childhood to manhood. By the time he gets out I am gonna be a man already and I hate it. I would write about this because it is important to me, and it's something big and dramatic.

As students get farther into their work, the reflections might revolve around how their reading is informing their writing.

> I was reading No Name in the Street by James Baldwin and I started thinking about the idea of just tell the story and let the reader experience it vs. guiding the reader with your own emotions and opinions (you had been talking about it in class) and I noticed the fluidity of Baldwin's writing. I think he found an extremely well balanced style of writing. He tells the story and states his ideas as well but he is so

articulate that he doesn't have to sell his thoughts, his ideas speak for themselves. I have no idea how long I will struggle to strike this kind of balance . . . probably all of my life.

Or they might discuss the techniques they are experimenting with in their writing.

I also tested out the "playing with time" technique you mentioned in class. I tried to view my memoir as a movie and right after the sentence, "I sighed and closed my eyes, thinking of the great task remaining before me . . ." (part of which came from The Gettysburg Address) I pictured the scene fade out and fade in with a scene that started in the past that revealed what the "great task" was.

Before they write the final reflection, we often brainstorm lots of questions and then group them into big categories they might want to write about. Here is a list developed by one of my classes.

Questions That Relate to Our Understanding of the Genre
How is memoir different from autobiography?
How has your perspective of memoir changed and/or deepened?

Questions That Relate to the Writing Process
Why did you choose the topic you chose?
What were the main problems you encountered? How did you overcome them?
In what ways did you revise your piece from first to final draft?
What was most enjoyable? What was least enjoyable?

Questions That Relate to Your Final Piece of Writing
What are the strengths and weaknesses of your piece?
How did you convey your memoir's central theme?
How do you feel about your final piece?
If you had more time, what changes would you make?

Questions That Relate to What You Learned About Yourself
What insights have you gained into who you were/are as a person?
How did your feelings about your topic change as you wrote?
What makes your memoir significant?
What effect has writing the memoir had on you?

Questions That Relate to People You Wrote About

How did/would people you wrote about react to your memoir?

How have your feelings toward people you wrote about changed?

Rather than asking students to provide a series of short answers to all of these questions, I encourage them to use the list as a guide to help them organize their thinking about what they have learned, what they are taking away. Here one student reflects on something that happened during the memoir writing process and how it affected her.

> I really didn't want my dad to read it, but he did. He found it in my room, and he wasn't going to read it, but he said that he just read the first bit, and he couldn't put it down. He came and talked to me about it, and he got so upset that it almost made him cry. I felt really bad. I was more upset about making him feel bad than the actual content of the memoir and the discussion. Except for one part. He said that the last thing he ever wanted to do was drive me away; that's what his mother had done to him. He said it would break his heart, and I knew it. He said he would do anything to prevent that from happening. I really didn't want him to read it and I sort of still wish he hadn't, but the fact is, we haven't fought as much since. I also realize that a lot of what I said in my memoir was exaggerated, and I focused on negative stuff way too much . . . Depending on what kind of mood I'm in, whether I'm feeling depressed or neutral, the writing can come out with such a different tone . . . I think that writing this memoir has reminded me one more time about how lucky I am. It sounds really corny, but it's true. I started out screaming into the computer about how miserable I was. Then I took out a few things, and added some others. In the end it was a much less angry piece of writing. I've come away with an "it could be worse" kind of feeling.

Penny, the author of *The Rice Bowl*, discusses how writing her memoir was a process of discovery and enabled her to get in touch with long-suppressed feelings.

> At last my memoir is complete. All of my feelings and emotions spilled out onto paper for the first time. Hopefully this is just the beginning of my journey to the hidden emotions inside of me . . . During the course of writing, I learned a lot about myself and about my family. I think this memoir brought the image of my family closer together and especially brought my mother and me closer. Writing my memoir I learned that I am definitely not alone to deal with my problems and that I will always have my family beside me. I discovered that finding a way to express my feelings would

make it easier than just bottling it up inside. Also I discovered that if I put my heart into what I'm writing, it can be accomplished successfully as I have done with my memoir.

The students' reflections open a window into their thinking, show me the progress they are making, and provide valuable information to guide individual or whole-class conversations.

WRITING CONFERENCES

Writing conferences are opportunities to meet one on one with students to see where they are and to have conversations with them about their work. Ideally, I would like to meet with each of my students several times during the course of the unit, but with over thirty kids in each class, this is logistically impossible. So I make sure to have at least one conference with each student, and then conduct follow-up conferences with the students that I think most need additional face time.

One of the most important things to remember during writing conferences is that we should be focused on helping the writer, not the piece of writing. It's often incredibly tempting to suggest specific ways writers can improve their pieces, but it is far more valuable to teach strategies that writers will be able to turn to every time they face whatever issues they are struggling with. I use a simple memoir conferencing sheet, with the student's name on top, the date of the conference, and then two prompts.

Writing Issue(s):

Strategies we discussed:

So after checking in with students, asking how things are going, I prompt them to identify something they are struggling with. I jot this down as the writing issue, and then we talk about strategies writers use when confronted with this particular issue.

"I have a few stories," a student tells me in a writing conference, "but I don't know how to organize and structure them into a memoir."

"Figuring out the structure can be tough," I agree, jotting down the writing issue he has identified. "What are some things writers might do in this situation?"

"Maybe just finish writing the stories and worry about connecting them later."

I nod and write that down. "What else?"

"Ask someone for help."

I smile and write that too.

"I guess I could just write about everything in the order that it happened."

"Chronologically," I say, nodding, and add that to the list. "Anything else?"

My student thinks for a moment. "I don't know."

I wait, giving him more time to think.

"Maybe I could do something like in the memoir you showed us the other day where he starts each story with a quote."

"David's memoir," I say, smiling. "You noticed how his stories were about a few different things and how he used quotes to provide a frame and make the whole thing flow. So you could come up with a linking device," I say, jotting this down. "Something that is consistent from story to story."

We look over the list of strategies together, and I think about what one new strategy I can teach my student to build his repertoire and give him another option for moving forward. "Something I've seen a few other students try," I say, "is making their stories work like stairs, with each story becoming more dramatic than the story before. It's sort of like a piece of music building toward a crescendo."

My student nods. "I could do that."

"It's something you could experiment with," I say, writing it down. "So what do you think you're going to try when you go back to your desk now?"

My student looks over the list. "Probably, I'll just try to finish the story I'm working on, but think about how to link it with the stories I already wrote."

As my student goes back to his desk, I make a note that I need to do a mini-lesson on this issue, since this conference was the third of the day in which it came up.

FIRST DRAFTS

Most professional writers work through many drafts of their books before those books are published. They get feedback from family and friends, from agents and editors; make changes small and large; put their work aside for periods of time and then revisit it with fresh eyes; and often end up with products that are vastly different from the first drafts they produced.

I require all of my students to submit completed first drafts of their memoirs, and I comment fairly extensively on each one. With each memoir being a minimum of ten pages, it is a punishing amount of work for me, even with a student teacher to read half the drafts, but I strongly believe that it is an integral part of the assessment and evaluation process. Through collecting and commenting on first drafts, I am able to do the following.

Make sure all of my students are keeping up with deadlines

With close to seventy students, some working in writers' notebooks, others on computers, it is difficult to gauge the exact progress of each student. I do weekly checks, but the first draft is the most concrete evidence I can gather as to whether my students are where they need to be in terms of how much they have written and how much effort they have expended, and whether the drafts are complete.

Identify any students who need more individualized support

I usually have a pretty good sense of this by the time students submit their drafts, but not always. Reading through first drafts, I get a clearer picture of who is on track and who is struggling. Some students know they are struggling but do not seek out extra help. Others think they are on track, but their work reveals major gaps in their understanding. Reading first drafts allows me to target certain students during the revision process and give them the support they need to be successful.

Encourage students by highlighting what each of them is doing well

Most professional writers will tell you that there are moments when they feel like everything they are writing is terrible, and student writers are no different. Having someone speak positively of your work goes a long way, so I always open my comments by highlighting something specific the writer is doing well. I never say something like, "Great job!" because this kind of general praise is not helpful and often dishonest. Rather, I might say, "The opening scene really grabs me because you use dialogue, descriptive action, and internal thought so effectively to let me experience what you were going through."

< 107 >

Provide at least two specific suggestions that students can incorporate as they revise

I want my students to understand that writers use feedback to improve their pieces of writing and that meaningful revision involves more than just making a few cosmetic changes. To this end, I provide students with at least two specific revision suggestions that require them to really dig back into their work. I also try, whenever possible, to word my comments in a way that speaks both to the specific memoir and to qualities of good writing in general. For example: "The opening scene works so well because you let us experience what happened rather than just telling us about it. Look for other places in your memoir where you can use dialogue, descriptive action, and internal thought so we can more fully experience the moment. In general, you want to show (not tell) the most dramatic or important or emotional parts of your story."

Identify common issues that many students are struggling with to inform future mini-lessons

When I find that I am offering the same two or three suggestions to many of my students, I know that this is an area that I should come back to in my lessons. For example, if many of my students could benefit from showing more and telling less, even though I have taught this concept already, I make sure to revisit it and give my students additional practice. If there are not issues that are so widespread, I note which students are struggling with the same issues and lead some guided writing groups after I have returned the first drafts.

Replicate the process by which a writer gets revision notes from an editor and then uses these notes to make the work better

I want my students' writing experiences to be as authentic as possible. Editors don't put grades on the manuscripts they get from their authors. They give the author notes that suggest ways to improve the work. And authors approach revision as thoughtfully and as diligently as they approach any other part of the process. As a teacher, I am just as interested in assessing my students' commitment to the whole writing process as I am in evaluating the final product they turn in.

Have a much better gauge on how to evaluate the students when they turn in their final drafts

Evaluating student work is always a balance between looking at process and product. If I were asked to grade a pile of memoirs from students I did not know, I would judge just the work in front of me. Fortunately, because I know my students and have read their first drafts, I can consider not just how good the final draft is, but also how far the writer and the piece have come during the drafting and revision processes.

Some Thoughts on Revision

I have to be honest. Convincing students to revise what they have already worked so hard on is a tough sell. Even the most motivated students often approach revision as a form of glorified editing, making minor changes—cutting a sentence here, adding a bit more description there—but shying away from truly reenvisioning their work.

I think there are a few reasons for this. The most obvious is that meaningful revision can involve a ton of work. What student wants to cut something that took long hours to write? Or come up with pages of new writing to replace what was cut?

Then there is the uncertainty of how to approach making major changes to the work. What exactly is required to develop the memoir's understory? How exactly does one go about showing more and telling less?

And finally, there is the issue of time. The drafting process lasted weeks, with many mini-lessons, large chunks of time to write in class, and mini-deadlines along the way to make it all seem more manageable. Revision is often something we ask the kids to do without providing the same structures and supports and class time that we provided during the brainstorming and drafting stages.

As a professional writer, I understand my students' reluctance. By the time I submit a draft of a manuscript, I have already done a ton of revision along the way. When I get notes from an editor, I am quick to embrace the easy fixes, but much slower to accept suggestions that will require major surgery. Are huge changes worth the time and effort? Will they really make the piece that much better? What if they actually make the piece worse?

Students attach value and importance to something in direct proportion to how much we, as teachers, seem to value it. If we give students two weeks to brainstorm, three weeks to draft, and only a few days to revise, we are sending a message about our priorities. If we provide many prompts and mini-lessons to support brainstorming and drafting, but only offer a single lesson on revision (you can add things, cut things, or move things around), we are sending a message about our priorities. The time students have to revise should last as long as the other stages of the writing process. It should be filled with mini-lessons and opportunities to experiment with strategies and techniques that writers use when they revise. And when we grade the memoirs, we should include the work the students did revising as an important part of our overall assessment and evaluation.

How I Grade the Memoirs

In a perfect world, you wouldn't have to assign a grade to such a deeply personal piece of writing. It seems awful to reduce everything the students have put into this project to a single grade. How can you tell a student who has written about the death of a family member that her work merits only a C?

On the other hand, students want a grade. It's the culture we have created in our hypercompetitive society. For many students, grades are the only things that motivate them to work hard.

I am not against assigning grades per se, but I do believe that we have to be thoughtful about how and when we give them out and extremely clear about what they represent. In the first place, students should know exactly what teachers are basing their evaluations on. These criteria should reflect what the teachers have been teaching and valuing in their classrooms and should be made visible to the students from the very beginning of the process. In a truly democratic classroom, teachers and students would determine the grading criteria together, and students would have an opportunity to evaluate their own work and the work of their peers.

In our school, rather than assigning letters or numbers, we describe student work as exceeding, meeting, approaching, or falling below standards. For projects, I use a rubric that I have created with some input from my students to describe the characteristics of work that falls into each of these categories. The memoir rubric is shown in Figure 8.1.

FIGURE 8.1

Memoir Rubric

AREAS OF EVALUATION	EXCEEDS STANDARDS	MEETS STANDARDS	APPROACHES STANDARDS	FALLS BELOW STANDARDS
CONTENT	You are very successful at opening a window into your life. You write about things that are very significant and meaningful and reveal a lot about who you are.	You are successful at opening a window into your life. You write about things that are significant and meaningful and the reader gets a good sense of who you are.	You are somewhat successful at opening a window into your life. It's not so clear what makes your topic significant and meaningful. You tend to focus more on the events of your story than on who you are.	A reader learns very little about you and your life from reading your memoir.
CRAFT	You skillfully employ techniques of good writing. You have a clear understory, you move effectively between the mountain and the sea, and you use language in powerful and sophisticated ways.	You incorporate techniques of good writing we have gone over in class. Your memoir has an understory, you move between the mountain and the sea, and your writing is clear and well organized.	You incorporate some of the techniques of good writing we have gone over in class. Your writing is not always clear, and there is no clear logic to the way it is organized.	You incorporate few or none of the techniques of good writing we have gone over in class. Your writing is unclear, disorganized, and reflects insufficient care and effort.
REVISION	You successfully incorporate the feedback you received on your first draft into your revision. Your final draft reflects significant changes and is a much stronger piece of writing.	You make a clear attempt to incorporate the feedback you received on your first draft into your revision. Your final draft is a stronger piece of writing.	You make some changes from your first draft to your final, but you do not really incorporate the feedback you received. There is not a significant difference between your first and final drafts.	There is no evidence of revision because you did not submit a first draft in time to get feedback.
MECHANICS	The piece reflects a command of the conventions of written English.	The piece reflects a solid grasp of the conventions of written English.	The piece reflects a partial grasp of the conventions of written English.	The number of errors makes the piece difficult to read and understand.
MEETING DEADLINES AND REQUIREMENTS	Your final draft was submitted on time and demonstrates extra effort and depth.	Your final draft was submitted on time and is at least ten typed pages.	Your final draft was submitted after the due date and does not meet the length requirement.	Your final draft was very late and is much shorter than the required length.

< 111 >

The rubric includes five categories and values both the writer's process and product. There is no final grade assigned, but based on what I underline, students are able to see the extent to which they exceeded, met, approached, or fell below expectations in each category.

I fill out a rubric for each student, and I invite each student to fill out a rubric for him- or herself. Many teachers consider self-evaluation an integral part of the evaluation process. I make it optional, because I know how uncomfortable it can be for students to grade themselves and because I have my students reflect regularly about their work throughout the unit. When my evaluation of a student's work differs greatly from the student's self-evaluation, I invite the student to have a conversation with me so we can share our thinking with each other.

Sometimes students will ask if they can do more work on their memoirs to improve their grades. In general, I will allow this, provided that they can do so without compromising other work they are responsible for. At times I feel frustrated that they did not put in more effort before the memoirs were due, but if they are willing to exert that extra effort now, I don't want to discourage them. It also frustrates me to know that their primary motivation is a teacher's grade, rather than their own pride and satisfaction in a job well done, but giving them every opportunity to see that with effort they can meet or exceed standards can transform students' attitudes about themselves and their capabilities.

✳   ✳   ✳

It is the end of the memoir unit, and we have turned our classroom into a theater of sorts. One by one, the students take the stage to share excerpts from their work. My student Lucy, the young woman who described writing her memoir as a way of unpacking the secrets she had long kept in boxes, steps up to read.

> *When I am young, I try to cut off my leg hair with scissors. This probably isn't the best idea, because I am left with patches of hair and stubble like I am on my first round of chemo. In middle school, I try again. I begin with nothing but water and my mother's 99 cent, pink drug store razor. Maybe just the ankles, I think. But ankles turn into calves, calves into knees and soon I am sitting on the rug smiling, rubbing my hands down what is sleek and smooth.*
>
> *My grandma is the only one to notice. We are sitting in her car, which is spotless and orderly. A Glade air freshener sprays French Vanilla sweetness in my eyes. She*

glances down and gasps. "You shaved your legs!" She hasn't looked this proud of
me since I learned to use a lint roller. It is then that I decide I am never shaving
again.

It is not easy, especially when I'm older. I watch the girls at camp congregate,
bringing their sacred Venus razors and mango shaving cream to perform ritualistic
"shaving parties." And even though I know they care, they nag me all the time to
come.

I learn to develop my own laws. Shorts? Completely off limits, as are dresses
without tights. Capris? Maybe in a foreign city. Maybe. By eighth grade, swimming
is out too. It's hard to trudge along in jeans in the sweltering heat and pretend
you're alright. It's hard to think of more and more excuses why you're doing so.

I watch my grandmother never miss an opportunity to introduce me to Nair,
Smooth Away or Veet. I watch myself reach into my stocking only to pull out
an electric razor. I watch the feminist movement disown me as they become more
concerned with the right of women to dress provocatively. I watch every other female
gallivant her way around in sundresses I wish I could wear, with long, smooth,
shiny legs, so perfect and flawless and feminine. I have those of a monster, a
mongrel, a man. The hair is rough and ugly, too gross to see the light of day like a
calling card from some infectious disease. No one can know.

But if it's so horrible, then why don't I just do it? Just take it off. A few flicks
of the wrist and, voila, I'm beautiful. In truth, it is not the shaving that bothers
me, but the fact that shaving is expected, that no one gave me any choice in the
matter, that people think this is the only way to be. I took the road less traveled
and I was punished. Continuing to do so was my form of protest. And while that
might sound strong, sometimes it just hurts too much. I cry whenever I am shown
kindness, and I can count on my hand the number of times this has happened.
Random people. A Korean nail salon owner, a camp counselor. Once, I am wearing
a dress we have nicknamed "the Sack." It falls limply around my body as the other
girls go through every tactic to make me put on something else. Until 18-year-old
Liana Blum walks in.

"I think she looks beautiful," she says.

And while this is incredibly touching to me, in the springtime, they still air
Venus commercials. "Release the Goddess in you," they say, because shaving
empowers women. Shaving makes them strong. The girls in the ads are twirled in
the air by the men who love them. "Our most touching moments . . . all start with

an embrace." I watch them lay on picnic blankets in someone else's arms. Laughing.
And looking into each other's eyes and up at the stars and down at her legs.

"Ugly," they tell me. "You're so ugly."

"You'll never be happy."

"No one will hold you this way."

"No one will hold you at all."

"No one will ever love you," they tell me.

"You're unlovable."

But after that reading, she is just the opposite, her classmates applauding loudly in awe and appreciation and support, recognizing that what she has shared, what she has bared, is, in fact, beautiful.

It is another magical moment, and when she approaches me after class and says she wants to keep working on her memoir even though the unit is over, it is a reminder that there are more meaningful and important ways to measure growth than anything you could learn from analyzing the bubbles on a standardized test.

CHAPTER 9

Struggling Students

About ten years ago my wife and I ran a workshop at Bank Street College about using personal writing with middle school students. I brought along a stack of memoirs my students had written and proudly displayed their amazing work. The teachers and principals, most of whom worked in less affluent school districts, were extremely impressed, but expressed serious reservations that their students could produce such high-caliber work. The general feeling within the group was that it was one thing to inspire this kind of work from the best students at a highly selective school like Salk, but something quite different when you were working with populations of students who were reading and writing below grade level.

The point is well taken. Each year, I have only a small percentage of students who score below standards on the state ELA exam or are at risk of failing my class, and it would certainly be more challenging to inspire such amazing writing if I were teaching in a different environment. On the other hand, when I think about the *reasons* I teach memoir writing, it's clear that these reasons are not at all specific to high-achieving students. In fact, it is easy to argue that the benefits of teaching memoir writing are even more pronounced for students who are struggling in school. When these students feel engaged, when they care about the work they are doing and see it as relevant and fulfilling, they demonstrate effort and commitment that might otherwise be lacking. When they have the opportunity to write about something they know, and recognize that their experiences lend themselves to powerful memoir writing, they are more likely to feel that the academic playing field has been evened out and that they can be successful. I think about the stories of Ryan, Ruby, and Alicia, and I know that writing memoir can have a transformative effect on students who are struggling in school.

Ryan

Ryan was part of a tightly knit group of five friends whom I grew to know better than most of my other students, because in addition to teaching them, I coached them for two years on the school basketball team and used them as the subjects of a never-finished young adult novel that I was writing at the time. In a taped interview session, Ryan described the group as follows:

> It's like something goes wrong in the school it's usually us that you think of or that a teacher thinks of because we're like kinda . . . we're goodfellas, we're good and bad, and, and, it's like if one of us was somewhere then you know another one of us was with him. Like we work together. But, you know, it doesn't bother me. I like the attention. We—we're like a rowdy group, I mean we're loud and obnoxious, but we're not stupid. We wouldn't go like rob somebody, but like we been thrown outta McDonalds, Toys-R-Us, the library, pizza places. We do things, but we do have our limits.

Ryan swaggered around the school as if he owned the place. He lingered in the hallway flirting with girls, was always at risk of failing several of his classes, and routinely got in trouble for causing disruptions.

At the same time, he was almost impossible not to like. Nothing he did was malicious, he always took responsibility for his behavior, and he was not ashamed to show that he was sensitive and vulnerable. In one interview session, Ryan spoke of the constant fights he had with his mom and how after each one he would lie in his bed and cry because he felt he was letting her down. He cried openly in school too, once in a conference with his mother and all his teachers, another time in the hallway after being sent out of math class.

Ryan's standardized test scores indicated proficiency in English and math, but he rarely did homework, had trouble staying focused in class, and had never made a serious effort to work up to his capabilities. "If there's one thing I wish I could change about myself," Ryan said in one interview session, "it's that I wish I could be more disciplined about my work and not be so lazy all the time."

The memoir unit did not transform Ryan into a model student, but when he was working on his memoir, I witnessed a level of focus and engagement that I had not previously seen. I watched him writing and rewriting, reading things he had written out loud to hear how they sounded, putting aside one section of writing to work on another, and wanting to talk to me about things he was struggling with. "I know what I want to say," he told me in one conference, "but I keep starting over because I want to make sure it's interesting to the reader."

After experimenting with different leads, Ryan settled on one he liked.

Can you remember the last time where you were alone to think and not be overwhelmed by your worries? The last time you sat alone in the dark and all you heard was the commotion outside and not the voices in your head? . . . . I do.

The opening resonated with echoes of our taped conversations earlier in the year in which Ryan had talked about lying in bed each night, trying to clear his mind of everything and just let his imagination wander. "It's like there's always so much going on—fights with my mom, me and my step-dad not talking to each other, my report card—at night I just want to think about girls and baseball."

When Ryan turned in a draft of his work about a week later, I was struck by the openness and candor with which he wrote about his life. I recognized characters and events from our interview sessions, but this was something much more than the stream-of-consciousness narrative that emerged on tape. This was a piece of fine craftsmanship—a coming-of-age story unfolding in interconnected scenes with reconstructed dialogue, humor, tension, and shifting levels of perception. At two key points in his narrative, for example, Ryan broke from his story and assumed a different, reflective voice, using italics to denote the break. In his own way, he was returning to our discussion about the sea and the mountain.

I reached out and put my fingers in the can. It felt really thick but when I withdrew my hands from the can it felt lighter. I looked down at my fingers covered in white. I felt this weird tingle in my body and I didn't want to be in the same apartment anymore. I lifted my fingers up to my nose. I took another look and quickly dusted the coke off my hands and put them in my pockets. Anthony put the bottom piece back inside, then put the whole can in his jacket and left. I sat there feeling weird not understanding why, not believing what just happened.

I didn't understand why I felt so guilty. I mean I didn't do anything wrong, did I? You know what's really bugging me though. I thought about sniffing it. For a few seconds there I thought about taking drugs. I know it sounds dumb, but I wonder what it would have been like to try some. Not a lot, just enough to get the feeling. Damn, I wonder if Reuben has ever done anything like that. I don't know how I'm going to be able to face him again.

Ryan uses this technique again at the end of his memoir, this time using the reflective voice to set up his powerful closing scene.

Obviously when someone in your family is dying it hurts. But it hurts even more when you were real close to that person. My uncle taught me how to do everything. He taught me how to play Nintendo, how to play baseball. He even taught me how to paint. He owned his own painting company called Painting with Pablo, and whenever he had small jobs he would take me with him and teach me one or two things. Me and him were so close and soon he won't even be here.

I spent all day laying in my bed like a bum. It was about 8:30pm and my brother came back from college to visit when he heard about my uncle. It was only me, him, my sister, and my two cousins in the house. I was watching t.v. in my mother's room when the phone rang. I was too tired to pick it up so I let my brother answer. About five minutes later he walked into the room.

"What's wrong Paul?" You could see hurt in his eyes. And in some way I knew what was about to come, I was just waiting for the words.

"That was mommy who just called from the hospital."

"Paul?"

"Tio just died Ryan."

My brother grabbed me and held me as I started to shake and cry. The words I was hoping he wouldn't say, he said.

"It's gonna be okay."

"No, it's not!" He's gone and he ain't comin' back!" I pushed my brother away and ran out of the apartment.

"Ryan come back!"

I ran straight down the hallway and up the stairs to the roof. I walked over to the edge and sat in the corner not being able to stop crying.

"Fuck. Why him? Why him?"

I need to get away. I can't be here right now. I grabbed the blunt Reuben gave me earlier. I couldn't stop shaking and crying. I pulled out a book of matches. I lit a match, and as I kept shaking a tear fell from my cheek putting the fire out before it even got started.

"What makes this memoir better," Ryan wrote in his second reflection, "is that the feelings are real so even if the student isn't a good writer you can still understand what the person is trying to make the reader see." He was pointing to something that has been echoed by students every year during our study. Memoir writing is more accessible than other genres because it is writing about what the writers know best.

Something else is at play, though, and that is a heightened sense of ownership. Because Ryan was writing about himself, he was vastly more committed to what he produced, putting forth extra effort to capture his own thoughts, feelings, relationships, and experiences and not shortchange himself as a complex and vibrant individual. Ryan embraced his memoir as a vehicle to grapple with his own identity and sense of self, and he emerged from the writing process with feelings of pride and academic accomplishment that had been in short supply throughout his middle school years. "The best thing I like about writing the memoir," he noted in his final reflection, "is that I learned a lot about myself."

Ruby

Ruby came to me with a warning from her previous teachers. Do not, under any circumstances, get involved in a power struggle with her. It was a challenge, considering the fact that she was almost always off task and was a disruptive presence at her table, talking and laughing and being loud. Unlike Ryan, she would almost always complete her homework on time, but there was no sense of engagement or true effort. Her attitude seemed to be, "I'm doing the work, so leave me alone." She was guarded and angry, and I worried about how she would react to the prospect of spending two months thinking deeply about her life and writing something as personal as a memoir.

As I had anticipated, things did not start well. Ruby, who always struggled to stay focused in class, was even more off task than usual, steadfastly resisting my efforts to get her writing and claiming she had nothing to write about even when I provided multiple prompts.

I finally sat down with her for a writing conference, determined to help her break through whatever it was that was keeping her from getting started. My objective in the conference was, quite simply, to find something—anything—that Ruby could start writing about. She was clear about the fact that she did not want to write a memoir, saying that her life was boring and that she would never be able to fill up ten pages. She had come up with a title, though. *Stupid Memoir.* It pretty much encapsulated her feelings about the whole enterprise. In fact, even after Ruby went through the process, eventually writing a powerful and moving draft and then making it even better when she revised, she still had this for a beginning:

> *Read another stupid memoir, one with a deeper meaning or perhaps a good title. Don't you have a goddamn booger you've been aching to pull out of your nose? Listen, this is not some comedy designed to make you feel all warm and fuzzy with witty charm. This is not some tale of tragic greatness there's NO-FUCKING-EPIC-ANYTHING here. So if you're looking for that, why don't you go pick up a book about a cuddly kitten and her cartoon friend? Nothing to see here.*

The power of the writing undercuts the message. Ruby might be saying that reading her memoir is a waste of time, but she makes it almost impossible to turn away because her voice is so dynamic. And, as it turned out, there was plenty to see, but it took some time for it to emerge.

I honestly don't remember what I asked that provided the first opening. All I remember was that I was patient, not allowing myself to become frustrated by Ruby's nonresponses to my questions, and showed real interest in any little thing she said. I had suspected that some of Ruby's reluctance to talk was because she did not want to share anything personal, but it turned out that this was not the case. The real barrier was that she was convinced she could never write ten pages and so she decided she wouldn't even try.

We had more conversations, and eventually, with lots of gentle prodding, she told me about quitting gymnastics, about her mother having a stroke, about being sent to group therapy sessions with much older kids.

"This is such powerful stuff," I told her. "Do you feel like you could write about all the things you've been telling me?"

She shrugged. "Not ten pages."

"Don't worry about the length," I said. "Just start writing."

And she did. Freed from the constraint of having to produce a set number of pages and reassured that her experiences were excellent material for a memoir, she poured out the story of her mother's stroke; of not getting any presents on Christmas; of living first with her aunt, then with her grandmother (who was afraid to go outside), then with her sister and her sister's boyfriend. She wrote about being in group therapy with a bunch of older kids who talked about sex and drugs and how it didn't help her at all. And on the day first drafts were due, she handed in considerably more writing than I had ever seen from her—nine typed pages—and said, with barely concealed pride, "I told you I wasn't going to write ten pages."

Ruby had never been one to spend time revising her work. Assignments, to her, were nuisances she needed to get done, and that was it. But her memoir had become something more to her, though she wouldn't admit to it, and when I commented on the many strengths evident in her first draft and the things she could do to make her piece even better, she offered only token resistance.

Since the content of Ruby's memoir was extremely strong, I pushed her to focus on craft, coaching her to transform the most dramatic parts into fleshed out scenes, complete with dialogue, descriptive action, and internal thought. I marked places where I thought she could do this, including the beginning where she tells about her mother's stroke.

The day after my mother's 49th birthday I decided not to go to gymnastics. I got home around five o'clock. My aunt and mom were sitting in her room talking. They had just gotten back from the doctor's office for a checkup. A week before, my

< 121 >

mom had gone to get bypass surgery . . . When my aunt left she said to call her if
anything happened.

My mom went into the kitchen to make dinner. Thump. I went in. My mom fell.
"What happened?"
"Nothing, I am fine," she said when she got up.
I went back to the living room and started watching television. My mom came
into the hallway.
"My side kinda feels numb." Rubbing her right arm.
"Are you sure you're alright?" I started to feel scared. The thought of my mother
dying or even being sick again terrified me. She had just gotten back from bypass
surgery in Florida and was due for a check-up on January 18. Plus she was the
one who took care of me, and where was I to go if she got sick? Would I have to
move to Florida to live with my grandmother, or move to Queens with my aunt? I
didn't want to live with anyone but my mother.
"Not anymore. Can you call the doctor?"
"OK. Where is the number?" As I searched her bag, my mom fell. When I
located the number she said to call the police. The police told me to get all of her
medicine ready for when they came. My mom was screaming that her head hurt
and rolling on the floor. By now, I was freaking out . . .

Ruby's ability to re-create this scene, and others, not only reflects her growth as a
writer, but also reflects her growth as a person. Through her memoir, she opened
up about a difficult period in her life and revealed her feelings of vulnerability,
something I had never before seen her do. She had also never volunteered to share
her writing with the class, but at the memoir celebration she stood in front of
the room and read an excerpt from her piece without laughing or telling people
to shut up or trying to sabotage the proceedings in any way.

I saw Ruby about seven months after she graduated. We had invited the
ninth graders back during Regents Week for a reunion, and she was one of
about fifty students who showed up. We had designated a classroom for the kids
to congregate, and I worked the room, greeting my old students, giving hugs,
asking about high school.

Soon students began drifting into the hallway, and when I followed them out
I saw Ruby standing by the benches in front of the office. I was glad she had
come, but the thought flashed through my mind that managing all the return-

ing students might now be more difficult with Ruby around. Would she respect the fact that classes were going on and she needed to keep her voice down in the hall? Would she seize the opportunity to act crazy since she was no longer a student in the school?

"Hi, Ruby," I said, walking toward her.

She smiled. "Hi, Jake."

I hugged her, and she hugged me back.

"How's high school?" I asked.

"It's boring," she said, but her voice was light, and she seemed happier, more comfortable in her skin than she had been in eighth grade. "Are you making your eighth graders write those stupid memoirs?" she asked.

"We'll be starting them soon," I said.

We stood a moment in silence, and then she said, "You can use mine if you want, if you need examples to show your class."

"Thanks," I said, and we exchanged a smile.

Alicia

Alicia arrived in my classroom on the first day of school looking like the grim reaper. Each day, shrouded in black, she would sit at her table and draw, either on her computer or in her sketchbook. When I assigned class work, she would fly through it, with little attention to quality, so she could return to her art. She never participated in discussions, though she assured me that she was paying attention. This assertion was undercut by the fact that most of the work she turned in bore only a slight connection to what we had been studying in class.

It was difficult to reach Alicia, because she seemed to care little about her grades and was generally uninterested in the curriculum. When I met her parents, I realized that they were at even more of a loss than I was. An elderly couple that looked far more like grandparents then parents, they had adopted Alicia as a baby and been unprepared for the dark and sullen teenager she had become.

When the memoir unit rolled around, I worried that Alicia would close herself off as she had been doing all year. But I suspected that if I encouraged her to create a graphic memoir, she might at least be more engaged and put forth more effort. I did not have any student models to show her, but I gave her David Small's *Stitches* (2009) and Marjane Satrapi's *Persepolis* (2003).

Alicia quickly confirmed what I had long suspected. Not only was she an extremely talented artist, she was also exceedingly creative and brilliant in a way that could not be measured by essay assignments or standardized tests. (I had seen this earlier in the year when, for a multigenre project, she had created a hysterically funny Facebook page for Death.) Now she aimed these creative talents at her own life, depicting her parents with one body and two identical heads, uttering words that perfectly captured their joint exasperation in trying to make sense of their daughter.

In the end, Alicia's parents mostly disappeared from her work, and she turned instead to her experiences in therapy, focusing on an incident in which her therapist questioned her sexual orientation (Figure 9.1).

There is so much that is remarkable about Alicia's work. Look just at the beginning of the first page. Notice how she jumps right into her story, hooking us immediately. Look at how her first picture cleverly plays off her opening words. Notice the subtle humor in wearing a shirt with a smiley face that says *FUN*, which completely belies her facial expressions and posture. And almost immediately she drops five little words that hit like a bombshell. Her arm runs into the edge of her first picture frame and, stunningly, emerges again in frame number three, a mostly empty box, with just her wrist dripping blood as she holds out her hand. Through pictures and words, Alicia reveals herself on the page—angry, vulnerable, depressed—giving voice to feelings she admits to keeping suppressed. But her work, though exploring painful subjects and serious themes, is infused with humor, so this angst-ridden adolescent emerges as a truly likable character, as does the angst-ridden author, who sits drawing in my class each day.

The memoir unit did not transform Alicia into a model student. In fact, after producing an incredibly promising first draft, she did not follow through with revisions, even though she acknowledged that there was still a lot she could do to make her piece better. But while she worked on her memoir, Alicia was more engaged, put forth more effort, and showed more pride than at any other point during the school year. At the memoir celebration, when I required students to share a short excerpt from their memoirs, Alicia brought hers up to the document camera, began reading from the beginning and just kept going and going until she had shared her entire work. The class was riveted, and wild applause followed her as she slunk back to her seat. Her head was down, but a smile creased the corner of her mouth.

Another magical moment.

FIGURE 9.1

Alicia's graphic memoir

It was apparently time for a therapy lesson; my parents thought I was too mental to handle being by myself. Incorrect. Just because I kept secrets didn't mean I was any more issued than the next guy.

I didn't cut myself then,

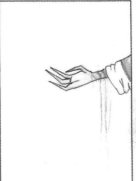

I didn't obsess over anybody then, I still don't but that's not the point.

I didn't yell at my parents to leave me alone back then either.

But I still hated going to my therapist. She bugged me so much... I couldn't talk to her without getting secretly pissed. She couldn't hear very well, so I had to almost scream my answers at her.

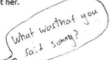

Well... Half of that was my fault; I always had a pillow over my face that I would refuse to take off.

My parents would drive me in a taxi over; we would all get out, walk into the building, and go up in the elevator, ring the buzzer, and wait in the waiting room. I would get called in and when I did, I rushed over to the couch and plopped myself down on it then cover my face with the pillow that was right by the front of the couch. It was an endless process of questions that I didn't feel like answering after that.

Today the first question after: "How are you?" Was: "So... Who do like in school?"

what?

How I
wanted to
respond...

Instead...

(I thought that people were not supposed to help eachother in those cases.)

I said quietly.

She pretended not to hear my answer. Either that or I was talking into the pillow again.

By now it was getting annoying. I didn't want to tell my *therapist* who I liked! How dumb am I to do so?! I mean... It was embarrassing.

So was her next assumption.

Appendix A: Modifying Instruction for Students with IEPs

When I wrote the first draft of this book, my entire experience teaching memoir writing had been in general education classrooms. But two years ago, I began coteaching a class where a third of the students have Individualized Education Programs (IEPs). In many ways, the experience has made me feel like a brand new teacher all over again. Of course we always have a range of abilities in our classrooms and should be finding ways to differentiate instruction, but in an Integrated Co-Teaching (ICT) classroom, the range of abilities can be considerably more vast.

The memoir unit, for all the reasons I have outlined in this book, has been one of the high points in our ICT classroom the past two years, but it has not been an unqualified success. I have witnessed the ways in which much of the work I have described is too advanced for my lowest performing students. I have had students who struggle to write complete sentences, much less identify and imitate specific craft techniques. I have had to scale back my expectations that all students effectively layer their writing with understory, or that they all submit memoirs that are a minimum of ten pages.

At the same time, I have seen that all of my students have experiences in their lives worth writing about and can benefit greatly—both personally and academically—from participating in the memoir writing process. I still have a lot to learn, but here are some emerging thoughts I have about how best to modify the memoir unit for students with IEPs.

All, Most, Some

Cornelius Minor, our former literacy staff developer from Teachers College, suggests a general framework for thinking about the planning we do in our ICT classes. What is it, he asks, that you want **all** of your students to know and be able to do at the end of a unit? He suggests that we place our most struggling students front and center in our minds when we list these objectives. Next, he asks us to list what we want **most** of our students to know and be able to do. These might be the grade-level skills and content understandings we have already established in our unit planning. Finally, he asks us to think about what we want **some** of our students to know and be able to do, pushing us to think about how we might challenge our high fliers, who often feel slowed down by all the extra scaffolding that filters into our instruction.

For the memoir unit, one of our objectives is for students to develop their skill in reading with the eye of a writer. It is unrealistic to expect all of our students to be able to do this equally well, but we do want all of our students to be able to access this skill on some level. So in our planning, we might differentiate our objective in the following way:

- **All** students, with teacher support, will be able to read short, carefully selected excerpts from both published and student memoirs, state what they like and/or don't like about the writing, and try out something they like in their own work.

- **Most** students will be able to read both published and student memoirs independently, discuss the strengths and weaknesses of the writing, and try imitating some of what they like in their own work.

- **Some** students will be able to identify a wide variety of craft techniques in both published and student memoirs, evaluate how well these techniques are being used, and experiment freely with these techniques in their own writing.

Another objective is for students to be able to uncover patterns and themes in their lives. Again, this will look different for students of differing abilities. Starting with what we can reasonably expect our lowest-level students to be able to do and then moving up from there, we might differentiate this objective as follows:

- **All** students, with teacher support, will be able to brainstorm memories, find different ways to group them together, and use these groupings to express something about their lives and/or who they are.

- **Most** students will be able to link together memories in multiple ways to highlight themes in their lives and reveal something meaningful about who they are.

- **Some** students will be able to uncover new insights about their lives and identities and illuminate these truths in deep and powerful ways.

Ideally, we should be using this kind of differentiation on a daily basis. But to start, try using it to think through your larger unit objectives. By redefining what success will look like for your most struggling students, you will make smarter decisions in planning and instruction and help everyone in your class participate in the unit in a meaningful way.

Content, Process, Products

Another way to think about modifying a unit of study is in terms of content, process, and products. In their book *Leadership for Differentiating Schools & Classrooms*, Carol Ann Tomlinson and Susan Demirsky Allan define these terms as follows:

> *Content* includes both what the teacher plans for students to learn and how the student gains access to the desired knowledge, understanding, and skills.

> *Process* is how the learner comes to make sense of, understand, and "own" the key facts, concepts, generalizations, and skills of the subject.

> *Products* refer to the items a student can use to demonstrate what he or she has come to know, understand, and be able to do as the result of an extended period of study. (2000, 7–8)

For the memoir unit, one way we can modify *content* for our lowest performing students is by having them read very short pieces of memoir writing, rather than full-length memoirs. One way we can modify *process* for these students is by providing the option of re-creating memories using art instead of writing. One way we can modify *products* for our most struggling students is by shortening the length requirement of what they submit. Thinking about differentiation in terms of content, process, and products provides multiple entry points for scaffolding the work we do in our ICT classrooms and helps us make more deliberate adjustments in our instruction.

Differentiated Rubrics

Another challenge we often face is how to evaluate students for whom we have made significant modifications. If we are differentiating the objectives we have for different groups of students, it follows that we should not be using the same rubric to evaluate everyone in our classes. One way to modify a rubric is to keep the same categories—in this case, content, craft, revision, mechanics, and project requirements—but use different language to describe what it means to exceed, meet, approach, or fall below standards. For example, under project requirements, a modified rubric might state that the final memoir needs to be three pages long instead of ten to meet standards. Under mechanics, it might say that the writer has proofread carefully for capitalization, rather than expecting the writer to have a solid grasp of mechanics in general. Under craft, it might say that the writer has included dialogue and narrative description, without mentioning understory or moving between the mountain and the sea.

With the memoir unit we have sought to make the categories broad enough that all of our students can access each category on some level. When this is not the case, however, an alternate way to modify a rubric is to eliminate certain categories for some students, or create new categories to align more closely with a student's IEP goals. It also makes sense to weigh categories differently for different students, again using a student's individualized goals to drive these decisions. Rather than operating from a one-size-fits-all perspective, we should always be using the knowledge we have of our individual students to drive the instructional choices we make.

Appendix B: Excerpts from Student Memoirs That Can Be Used as Models

Providing models of outstanding student work is essential in teaching the memoir unit. Ideally, these models should come from your own classroom, so that students feel a closer connection to the work they are doing and recognize that the wonderful memoirs they are reading have emerged from the very classroom in which they are sitting. For teachers who are teaching the unit for the first time, or who have not yet built up their own library of student work, here are excerpts of memoirs from my classroom that reflect some of the best writing I have seen over the years.

There are certain topics that appear frequently in the memoirs, and it is useful to have models to hand students who are grappling with how to write about these issues.

Self-Image

FROM *PROM SHOES*

When I looked into the mirror I didn't like anything I saw. I hated all of it. After a while I took the mirror out of my locker because it was no use, I would still look ugly no matter how much I fixed myself up. Mirrors were my enemy. When I looked into them I saw a fat round face painted in the ugliest shade of brown with a humongous nose right in the middle of it all which was placed on a short neck connected to a round, lumpy, blubbery body. Not to mention the frizzy unmanageable hair and ugly clothes. All my bad features stuck out at me and covered all the good things . . .

When seventh grade began, I didn't even try to be pretty like I had done the year before. I told myself that I was ugly and there was nothing I could do about it. I deserved to be ridiculed and I deserved to cry. I don't know why I thought this because I know I was smarter than this. I guess there comes a time when a person has had enough they begin to believe the things everyone says about them. I guess that's what I did. I believed that I was hideous and that the only girls that were

< 136 >

*pretty were the skinny girls with light skin and silky hair. I made myself believe
that the things I saw in movies or on TV were really true. For a while I believed
that no one would ever love me and that I was destined to grow old by myself. I
believed all these things but I did not want them to happen. I was angry at god
for making me look as I did. Why couldn't I be skinny and white? Why was it me
who had to look so different? I began to spiral downwards and all I wanted to do
was fall in a deep dark hole and be left alone forever. And that's when it happened.*

*After a while of just crying every day and every night, waking up to find my
pillow still wet with tears, I was eager to change the way I looked. I never had an
appetite anymore and I refused to eat anything but packaged food that showed the
calories on the side. I ate barely anything. Most days it was just a couple of crackers
and juice. I bought this diet green tea thing that was supposed to make you have no
appetite at all and believe me, it really worked. I had horrible stomachaches and often
felt sick because of drinking it, but I still drank it. I counted every calorie I ate and
if I thought I ate too much I would try to make myself throw up. Then I would cry
and cry. I exercised a lot and my stomach became hard and flat. Slowly the pounds
began to drop. Slowly at first, by 2 pounds and 3 pounds, and then by 5 pounds and
6 pounds, but it wasn't fast enough for me. I wanted to be pencil thin because that's
what would fix all my problems and make people like me more. Even after losing 20
pounds I was not happy and saw myself as a big boulder. Still I cried and cried and
cried day after day. The weather was getting warmer and I was still isolating myself
and pulling myself back into the dark hole where I thought I belonged. I never called
back when people called me, and I always cut phone calls short. I didn't go out much
with my friends. I just wanted to be alone. Soon my hair began to fall out and I
could see bald spots forming in certain places. I didn't let myself have any fun because
I was too obsessed with my appearance. Too critical of every single thing about myself.
I became weird, someone who I never thought I would be. When I met new people I
would compare myself to them and then pick out what they had that I didn't have.
I would just think about who was prettier than who, and compare one person to
another person, and then to me. It was an obsession . . .*

FROM *PITY*

*Pretend my life is a movie. Like Being John Malkovich. I am John Cusack. A
nobody puppet master on the outside, and a tormented soul on the inside. If only
anyone cared.*

There are several scenes that never make it to my film.

The first scene:

Teacher: "Here are your tests, children."

Teacher hands out papers. Students receive them quietly, frowning before they even view their grades. They don't say a word. They're all too busy thinking of excuses for their parents. These students sit in rows. Quiet little rows.

"Thank you, teacher." That's the preppy student sitting in the middle. This student has two straight rows of teeth and two blue eyes. This student wears two perfectly white shoes with two perfectly tied laces. This student has two clean little hands with ten grown and groomed fingernails lightly painted with tainted blue dye. Two arms lay crossed atop of this student's shining desk. This student wears frilly white socks and clean blue jeans and a conservative little striped shirt. To match the shirt, this student wears two neat, blonde braids, tied faultlessly with striped bows. This student is me.

A sigh. A sigh of relief. From me.

"Another hundred, huh?"

A sigh of exasperation from a frowning student to my right.

"Hundred and two."

"Smartass."

"Shush! The teacher will hear you!"

A sigh.

Another sigh.

"Why you gotta be so smart?" This from the frowning student to my left.

"I'm not smart. I studied."

"Studied what? The dictionary?"

"A little . . ."

"Oh, you're kidding me."

"What? What is wrong with that?"

"Nothing. Nothing."

Frowning student to my left turns around. Frowning student to my right has long ago lost interest in marveling over my grades. I'm just the preppy student from the corner again. The teacher's pet with the perfect little teeth and eyes and shoes and hands and socks and outfit and hair and whatnot.

I think about how much I hate what I am. And I think about threats I could make. I'll be less preppy if I don't match my socks tomorrow. Then they'll laugh at you. *I'll leave my hair a mess tomorrow.* Then you'll look like a fool. *I'll insult the teacher tomorrow.* Then you'll get expelled. *No!* Prep. *I'm not a prep!* Then insult the teacher. *No!* Sissy. *I won't do it.*

Then, right when I am on the brink of tears, I begin to pity myself. How sad that I argue with myself. How sad that I study from the dictionary for a fourth grade spelling test. How sad that I am afraid to use a curse. How sad that I have perfect little teeth and eyes and shoes and hands and socks and outfits and hair and whatnot. How terribly, miserably sad.

Parent-Child Relationships

FROM *PEOPLE PERSON*

One day, a dark and rainy day, my mother called me, no beckoned me, no summoned me to her room. She sat me there, patted me on my head and told me, "Get dressed dear, we are going to meet your other Mommy." The day my mother told me she had a girlfriend did not happen this way. But it may as well have:

"Jade, can you come in here for a second?"

Oh no. Oh God no. That voice. That earnest, stern, ominous voice—the one I call her 'teacher voice.' It was, still is, and probably always will be the very thing that makes me know I'm about to have an uncomfortable conversation. Excuses, Jade, excuses. I can't start bleeding, I can't run away, umm . . . what to do?

"Hold on, I'm in the bathroom!" Okay, I have two, maybe three minutes, and I have to face the Voice.

"Hurry up, this is important."

Yeah, like I didn't already know that.

"Kay."

She is on her bed, I am at her door. I do things, squeak the door, tap my foot, click my tongue, try to make it less awkward. I don't.

"What are you doing?"

"Nothing. What do you want to talk about? My best strategy now is just to get through it as fast as possible.

"Okay, Jade, this might be a little weird for you."

How do I respond to that? Like what does she want me to say? Yeah, it will be.

"Okay. What?"

"Well, I am a people person. I like all different types of people. Tall people, short people . . ." Okay, where are you going with this? Let's get on with it . . . *"and fat people and skinny people, and Asian people and black people. Sometimes I like people because they are my friends. Sometimes they are like family. Sometimes they are more than that though. Like, the way I felt about your dad when we had you. And the way I felt about John when I was with him. Do you understand?"*

"Yes."

"And sometimes I like people like I liked Daddy and how I later liked John even when I don't care what gender they are. Do you understand that?"

Oh. My. God. Breathe in, breathe out.

"Okay."

What do I do? What do I do? Oh my god. I'm scared and angry, confused.

"Okay."

"That's it? You don't have any questions? Nothing that makes you sad, or angry, or confused?

"Nope."

You just told me something that will shape my life, and yours forever. My mother is with a woman, and you need to tell me this now? Why? Why now? Why are you telling me this at all? Why can't you be normal? Why can't you just be with Daddy? Or even, eww, John? Why are you so selfish? Why can't you think about me? How am I going to tell people? How am I going to tell Daddy? Why are you doing this? Wait? Are you okay, Mommy? Do you feel alone? Are you scared? What are we going to do? What are you going to do?

"What do you mean, okay? Are you sure you're okay?"

"Yeah."

Maybe things would have been different, though, if in that precise moment I answered differently. Let her in and shared. I might have lived with a little less worries, a little less anxiety.

She wasn't happy: she wanted me to be curious, and, well, normal. But I wasn't. I couldn't be. Because I'm not willing, am never willing to let her see that. To let her think that she may have screwed me up. Because if she knew that, if she knew

< 140 >

the things I thought about and worried about, she would never forgive herself. I couldn't let that happen, so I let it be. And told her I was fine.

FROM *MISSING HOMELAND*

When I was little, from an infant until I was four, I lived in China. Without my parents by my side, I had my grandparents. They were like my replacement parents. My parents were on the other side of the earth. 3000 miles away in a place they called America.

"Then what am I doing here?" I once asked my grandma.

She told me my parents were coming to bring me there, where I would get to see them every day. I was excited. Waiting for that day to come made me more and more eager. When would they come?

When they did come, least expected, everything changed. They were strangers to me. Strangers whom I belonged to. They took me on a plane, flew 3000 miles to a stranger's place. So different from where I used to be. Before this, I had dreams of a happy family living in a bug house with a garden and pretty flowers everywhere. Everyone's dream of a family . . .

It was the middle of the night and I really needed to pee. I would usually wake my grandma up to go with me, but since she thought I was such a trouble maker, waking her up would only make the situation worse. I was scared of the dark and the giant cockroaches that crawled in the shadows. When I was not looking one might even take a big bite out of me. I had to have someone to go with me, but who?

Not Grandma. Uncle? No! Grandma had told me I was a girl and he was a guy. Grandpa and Ba ba? Same reason. Mei mei? She still wore diapers. Ma ma? She was the only choice I had. I walked down the hall into the guest room quietly and quickly, afraid I would encounter any big roaches. Everyone in the room was sleeping peacefully, except for Ba ba: he was snoring so loud. I shook my mom lightly. In an instant she was awake.

"What happened?" she asked in a whisper. Her eyes weren't fully awake. I told her I had to pee. She got off the bed, put on her slippers, took my hand and led the way to the bathroom. It was a cold night so I leaned closer to my ma ma. I felt the warmth of her.

"I can't sleep. Can you tell me about America?" I asked her.

She tucked me tightly with the blankets. "Hm . . . let me see. How about I tell you about the food they have there. Have you ever heard of McDonalds?"

"Nope. What's Mc-Doe-na-as?" I said weirdly. She laughed at my pronunciation, but I didn't mind.

"It's a fast food place. They have hamburgers and fries, and chicken mcnuggets."

I moved to a side for my mom to sleep next to me. We both faced each other and I continued to talk. "When you go back to America, can you bring me back some of those foods?"

"Little silly, I don't have to bring the food back here. We can all go to America and have McDonalds."

"Huh?" I asked. I didn't understand what she meant by we all go to America and have McDonalds. I was not going to America. I was about to ask, but Ma ma cut me off by telling me a bedtime story.

"Let me tell you about a frog prince. Once there was a princess. The princess was a very selfish person and always thought she was better than everyone else . . ." I moved closer to Ma ma. She smelled good, like sunflowers. She sounded like a sweet lullaby as she told the story.

"The frog prince followed the princess. He kept asking for her hand in marriage . . ."

I closed my eyes and fell asleep.

FROM *CONTINUATIONS*

There's a small girl and a man. The girls looks about 5, maybe 6. Their backs are to you. You wonder if the girl, with her short stature, and bouncing golden curls, might be Shirley Temple. When she doesn't break into a tap dance in the next five minutes, you realize she's not. The man's taller, and in the silhouette of his outstretched arm, you see her skinny arm, the two arms form a 'V,' and where they meet you see a large fist of the man, where, you assume, the girl's hand is hidden, safe inside.

The little girl is me. I look up at my father who smiles down at me, and gives my hand an affectionate double squeeze, which between us, has wordlessly come to mean, "I love you." His smile reaches up on either side of his face, daring to touch the sky. The smile lines on his eyes are in synch with his mouth, and all the stray wrinkles, that were once without purpose, run, like paper clips to a magnet, to the epicenter, which is his corner eye. From there they fan outwards, and add age to his almond-shaped hazels . . .

I want to be like Alice, who lives in her own world of friends and foes and crazy hatters. Who can eat a mushroom or wander around a cave, and have her life change in an instant. I crawl below the mushroom, and underneath the bronze is cool. Small bronze animals surround me. My dad crawls next to me, and though seemingly awkward, he slides right in. With dad here now, I become one of the bronze animals, or maybe the animals become us. The lines between bronze and flesh, night and day, cold and hot, merge. They become something that's all of them, and nothing at the same time. We live in an alternate reality, where time doesn't exist for us or anybody else. Our bodies don't belong to us anymore, and our new ones are weightless. We don't want to know what we look like, and if we did we couldn't, because everything changes so fast our appearance can't keep up with us. Things like gravity that are dulled, are amplified in other ways. You know things, without having to realize them, and all that's there are concepts and emotions that float like thick, white clouds in the air around us.

Soon we hit the trees. Cherry blossoms fill one tree. With wide-set branches, we climb up, and lean back. Almost instantly I'm with Bobo the gorilla. I've come to visit him in the jungle.

"I brought you a backpack full of red bananas," I tell Bobo, because they are his favorite, and rare in the jungle.

"Oo oo ah ah," my dad says. If any tigers or animals threaten Cassie, Bobo swings them over his head, beats his chest, and banishes them from the animal kingdom forever. We eat cashew nuts and climb down . . .

We walk, my hand in his, down the cement roads of Central Park. I look up at my dad, and think of how many days we spend playing together in this park. I think of making artwork with chalk on the sidewalk, I think of watching him build me a treehouse. I think of my grandparents' faces when he tells them he doesn't want to take a job, that he wants to stay at home with me. I think of turning over rocks in the woods, seeing what creatures live beneath.

We stroll out of the park, and into the busy streets of New York City. Sirens sound, cars rush, the sour smells of garbage, urine, and car exhausts fill the air. I feel the warmth from his hand inside me, irremovable, following me always, as we step into the concrete jungle.

Divorce

FROM *JIGSAW*

I look down to the street. Mom and Dad are yelling. If they were on the lawn speaking in normal voices they would be barely audible from the room, but because my parents are screaming, every word they say can be heard. Eight-year-olds normally do not hear their parents screaming vulgarities at one another, but now mine speak freely. It's almost as if they want us to hear what they are saying.

I stand on my toes peering out the window and listening. It's like a Spanish soap opera; yells, screams, cries, and accusations are being thrown from one person to the next. A man who I have only met once, Jorge, is standing next to my mother with his hand on her lower back. I do not want to hear any of this, and I do not want to see any of it so I walk over to the bed and lie down between E.D. and Tilly [my cats]. I had always thought that things between my parents would work out, but now seeing them screaming, and seeing Jorge standing there, I know that nothing will ever be the way it used to be again.

After the throats of my parents are sucked dry, Mom walks into the house. I remain looking out the window at Dad. He walks around in circles muttering under his breath and kicking a rock on the ground. Eventually he turns to the house, takes a huge breath and walks to his car. Dad takes the keys out of his pocket and jams them into the door to open the car. It beeps. He opens the door and gets inside, then he slams the door as loudly as I've ever heard and drives away, shooting down Wolves Lane.

I hear Mom walking up the stairs toward her room, so I leave and walk to her office. I pick up the phone and dial.

"Hi Melissa, it's Ella," I say with a shaking voice.

"I'll get Sophia for you. Are you okay?" responds Melissa.

"I'm fine. Thank you."

The line goes still for a moment and then Sophia picks up the phone. "Hi," says Soph.

I break down. Sobbing, I say, "Sophia, my mom and dad just got in a huge fight in the street. They were screaming, I'm sure you could hear it, and this guy was there, and at the end of it my dad got in his car and drove off. He seemed really mad. I don't know if he's ever coming back."

When I was seven I thought my life was going to be the way it had always been. My life was supposed to be like everyone else's who I knew in my small, secluded suburb. My parents would stay married and be in love for the rest of their lives . . . Unfortunately my life has turned out to be the opposite of what I imagined. Nothing in my life is as I said it would be when I was half the age I am now, and although I'm perfectly happy with who I am, I frequently look back and say, "Hey, why isn't my life like that?" Neither of my parents ever told us why they split up, making the whole thing a book that will never be closed.

FROM *THE LAST PLACE HE STOOD*

After my parents' divorce my father took off and left me behind; I never got a birthday card, or any recognition of my existence, but I learned to live with it. At this point I was five. Seeing as I was fairly young when my parents split up, I never really got to know my father like the other kids I knew.

I would often sit on my bed and wonder about him, what he was like, was he smart or rich or funny? Sometimes I thought about him being a doctor, or someone in the government. But my father did not fit any of those descriptions. When my mom met him he was a busboy at the Waldorf Hotel, but many times I chose to disregard this fact, because that's what I wanted to believe and that's what I wanted my friends to believe, so that's what I told them. These little white lies became my comforts because they made anything possible.

Eventually I gave up on my father and I started to tell people he was dead. I didn't see any harm in it because I never saw him. I didn't just say he died though; I would make up extravagant deaths, ones that gathered sympathy, but in the end it was the easiest way to tell the other kids I didn't have a father.

I remember one time in 3rd or 4th grade some girl started asking me about my father.

"Where's your father?" she asked me out of nowhere.

"I don't have one," I said, trying to avoid the topic.

"What do you mean you don't have one. Everyone has a father. How else would you have gotten here?"

"Well my parents are divorced so I never see him."

"Oh, well, he probably doesn't love you anymore, that's why he left."

"No, he loves me."

"Then why don't you ever see him?"

After that last remark I ran to the bathroom, sobbing and thinking about what the girl had said. I was trying to reassure myself, he did love me I thought, I mean didn't he? I was full of questions and things I'm not sure I had thought about until that girl had mentioned my father to me.

I knew my life wasn't like everyone else's; I always stayed after school because my mom was always at work, and I barely ever got picked up from school when it ended. I lived in a house with my aunt and my grandmother, and it's true I was missing a father, and I wanted one more than anything, because I wanted to be like everyone else . . . I hated overhearing stories the other girls told about their perfect wonder-bread families. Sometimes I thought about being adopted and having a new life without any memory of the past. Sometimes I thought about just running away, but I stayed with my mom. I already knew what it was like without a father, how could I rob her of a daughter?

FROM *LEFT ALONE*

"I can't take this anymore!" my dad murmured to himself when he looked at my mother on the phone. I looked at my father, and looked at my mom. I knew what he couldn't take anymore. My mom was always on the phone or watching television. As long as I could remember, when I came home from school I would see her either watching soap operas or talking on the telephone. When I would ask her what was for lunch or for dinner, she would say, "I don't know" or "check in the freezer." . . .

"I can't take this shit anymore!" my dad said . . . "Get off the fucking phone . . . NOW!" I saw my father grab something and throw it across the room. As soon as I heard the object hit the wall, I jumped. My mom jumped too.

"Listen I have to call you back, okay? Okay, bye. Now what do you want?" my mom said with an attitude. I always thought that my mom considered herself a better person than my father. Her family acted the same way.

"I don't want you on the phone."

"What the hell you mean you don't want me on the phone?"

"You're on the phone too damn much."

"Well excuse me if I have friends to talk to and I have nothing else to do."

"Why don't you find something to do?"

"What do you want me to do . . . clean?"

"Yeah, you can clean."

"What the fuck . . . clean . . . this damn house is spotless. I busted my ass this morning and afternoon cleaning this fucking house. There's nothing to fucking clean."

I looked around my room; things were in place, dirty clothes were in the laundry, and even my bed was made. Shit, my bed was never made. My mom had a point.

"Well, you can read . . . just do something else besides being on the fucking phone!" My dad's voice became louder.

"If you don't like what goes on in my house, then maybe you should leave."

"Your house! This is my house . . . I'm the one who's paying the fucking bills, not you . . ."

"My name's on the lease, so it's my house too."

While I was listening to them arguing I got scared . . . After the argument, my dad stormed out of the house. I ran to my window and saw him look at me and whisper, "Bye, princess." Being my eight-year-old self, I stupidly thought he would come back in a few minutes. The minutes became weeks. I remember saying to my mom, "Mommy, where's Daddy going?"

"Don't worry, honey, Daddy will be back. He's going to the store."

I believed my mom; I never thought that she would lie to me. When my father left, questions and thoughts roamed my mind. Where did he go? Why did he leave? Was it me that made him leave? If it was something that I had done, would he forgive me? Then I started to think about all the bad things I had done that month. Did he find out about the fight I had? Or did he find out about the time I forgot to do my homework? Or was it that I got detention for something I didn't do? And the last question that I wondered was when is he coming back?

When my dad finally did come back he said he would never leave again and I believed him . . . I was wrong.

School

FROM *THE BITTER/SWEET BOX OF CHOCOLATES I CALL MY LIFE*

"Push your chair in and you may go." The teacher dismissed us.

The monotonous droning of the lesson was over. A clatter of metal moving across the floor tiles filled the room. Chatter erupted from almost every student that had been holding in a comment since it came to them some time during the period. I scribbled down the most recent assignment in my homework planner. I watched my peers swing their backpacks crammed with notebooks, folders, and textbooks from different classes over their shoulders and file out of the room.

"What do we have after lunch?"

"Science," I replied simply.

I was reliable that way. I could be asked and I would know, but after the inquirer groaned the conversation was over.

Without looking up from my bag the silence indicated the room was now empty. Feeling forsaken I left the classroom quickly to enter the hallway abuzz with chatter. I stalled at my locker placing and replacing books in my bag. Everyone was pulling out their food from home or their out-lunch passes and wallets, because now it was the time where you would either go to the nearest deli or pizza place to hang out with your friends, travel farther to find your favorite cuisine or go downstairs to hang out in the courtyard, because it was lunch. This was the worst part of my day. I dreaded science, gym was tiring and I felt insecure in math, but lunchtime remained the worst part of my day. At lunch you found out who your true friends were if you had any at all. You could sit next to someone in class and not be able to shut up or quit passing notes, but that did not guarantee you a lunch buddy. On a field trip you could be playing hand games, sharing a subway pole or seat and be altogether inseparable, but the next day it could be forgotten and mean nothing. There were too many people who had come from the same elementary school. Too many people who had knit together a tight circle of friends in 6th grade, a group of friends that was not letting in any more members and I had been in and out of these groups too sporadically to be able to call one my own. It was much too scary to go out to lunch. Enough people knew me that I could not sit in the park and be invisible, but not enough people liked me for me to feel comfortable tagging along with them . . . that's how I began spending my lunches wandering up and down the hall, but because there were only two floors and three different staircases it wasn't long before some teachers wondered why I was walking by their door for the fifth time in twenty minutes, though most didn't notice me.

Now there was this fellow classmate who was as close to my sworn enemy as you get when you're not in cinema's latest superhero movie. You have to understand she didn't immensely dislike me. She hated me. Therefore I hated and feared her. I don't know if there was an exact moment when we went from acquaintances to combatants. It's highly likely it was when she spilled water on my chair and convinced at least five people that I had peed in my pants. I knew she would use any situation that could even possibly embarrass me (as she had come to understand humiliation was my Achilles heel) as ammunition. She had seen me wandering the halls once before and called me a "retard who can't even find her class" in her loud booming voice that echoed throughout the hall.

So there I was putting in the combination for my locker for the third time when I heard the voice that gave me the sensation of a thousand cockroaches crawling up my back. I quickly abandoned my locker and slipped into a less commonly taken staircase. I got halfway down the steps and thought I was safe when I heard a door open above me. I rushed down the rest of the stairs and paused while wondering where to go. My legs were ready to run, but I had no safe place to go. I heard two other voices with her; with an audience I knew more of my self-esteem was at risk. I felt the thudding in my chest triple in speed. I ducked my head and slinked into the back stairwell. If I stood in the exact center of the middle landing I had a chance of not being seen. The only thing I was afraid of was them being able to hear me panting like a dog. I heard all six of their feet hit every twenty-four steps going down the stairwell. I stood there, breathing heavily, waiting, hearing their footsteps fade as they descended until I was sure they had reached the first floor and were out of the building then I leaned against the staircase wall and slid down, feeling the cool of the metal on the bare part of my back between my pants and shirt. My heartbeat and oxygen intake slowly returned to normal. I sat listening to the sound of my own breathing. I waited for what felt like forever and checked my watch to see if lunch was over yet. I still had a whole half an hour. Thirty minutes. One thousand and eight hundred seconds . . .

FROM ME, LADY PHILOSOPHY?

From age three to eleven, I walked with my mom from the 77th Street and Lexington subway station to 79th and Madison. Every morning we passed by fancy boutiques, overpriced coffee shops, art galleries and doggy accessory shops. When we saw the bronze plaque for the Iraqi embassy gleaming in the morning light we knew we were two steps away from 12 East 79th Street, officially known as Abraham Lincoln School.

When we turned up the stone steps and entered the heavy oak door, the statue "Lady Philosophy" greeted us each morning. She was everything we were expected to aspire to. This tall, brass woman, roaming in a beautiful garden with hands outstretched, represented wisdom, serenity, and the true Self. She was everything *the school wanted to show us about self-realization and inner beauty. The stunning image of her was a reminder to us all of our inner perfection.*

Just past her were the dark wood walls with intricate carvings and crystal chandeliers hanging from the ceilings. Surrounding her were spacious classrooms with glass paneled doors, oriental rugs, symbolic framed paintings and hardwood floors. Above her were the ideas of ancient philosophy. Hidden around her, though, was inevitable failure . . .

I was late to assembly again. I couldn't find my knee socks. This meeting of the whole school consisted of a philosophy lesson, singing and Sanskrit prayers. I quietly turned the glass doorknob and opened the door. The curtain flapped behind me, blowing cool wind on my face. I heard all of the children chanting, "That is perfect, this is perfect, take perfect from perfect and the remainder is perfect, peace, peace, peace" in Sanskrit and shut the door. Quickly I ran to an empty spot in the floor, my bare feet in my shoes squeaking, and sat down. We continued on with the Lord's Prayer as I felt Mrs. Scott's hot glance on my feet. Then she discreetly tapped Mr. Sanders and shot me a look. He recited the rest of the prayer methodically, watching my feet squirm under his scrutiny. Once the prayer was over he held up his hand. I was motioned to stand, and every pair of eyes was on my feet. Then Mrs. Scott flicked her hand at me to leave, and Mr. Sanders said not to come back. This was enough to show me how disrespectful I was and how ashamed I should feel. I inched upstairs back to the room I had been in moments before. I thought to myself: How could a pair of socks upset them so much? If the thing they strived to teach me the most was that I was perfect on the inside, then how come without socks I couldn't even be in their presence? How could my clothes make me a bad person? Then, through eyes blinded with sadness and shame, I saw my navy blue knee socks hanging off the edge of a bookshelf and didn't bother to put them back on.

Racial Identity

FROM *CONFESSIONS OF A TWINKIE*

Sometimes, when I'm on the bus, I pretend to be white. Lighter skin would make things so much easier. No assumptions about math, rice, nail salons. On the bus I will enter an alternate world. One where the people around me think—"white girl. White skin. Blue eyes, big eyes. Blonde hair." I wish. I look out the window. Look down. My hair is still black. Sigh.

People call me the atypical Asian—one who is bad at math, one who eats rice with a fork, one who doesn't live in Chinatown. I call myself an honorary white. My two Asian friends call me a Twinkie or a banana—yellow on the outside, white on the inside. I like this. I don't want to be the stereotypical Asian. I am American. I was adopted by white parents. I assimilated before I turned one year old. Then why do people associate me with math, rice and squinty eyes? I have a math tutor. I hardly eat rice. My eyes, for an Asian, are large. So I try to act the opposite of Chinese stereotypes. Asians are good at math? Math is my worst subject. (It actually is, no joke.) I get low grades on math quizzes. I fail to participate in math. I complain about the subject.

I am not good at math.

Asians eat rice with chopsticks every day? I never eat rice unless we get takeout Chinese food, which is about twice a month. Even then I eat it with a fork.

I do not eat rice with chopsticks.

Asians have small, squinty eyes? Look at mine. People say they're large, for a Chinese person anyway.

I do not have small, squinty eyes.

I am not the stereotypical Asian.

Repeat five times until you get it straight.

FROM *LEAN WIT IT ROCK WIT IT*

Just to make it clear I can do the "Lean Wit It Rock Wit It." It's a new dance that came out from Dem Franchise Boys that anyone who is black or Latino is required to know. I can do it but I find it hard to do in front of people because at school I've been labeled white. Someone like Snoop Dogg can put on a shirt and tie and a knitted sweater and still be called black. I can try everything to prove that who I am is actually black but I'd still look like a joke. Ever since kindergarten when I started noticing that I was different in terms of color and race compared to others, I've been changing and molding myself to the cultures and people around me. Even today I have two personalities: I can act one way in my neighborhood where I'm cutting out syllables and saying things like, "I'ma deck that niggah in his fucking face, he thinks I'm playing with him." I've been acting white for so long in school that if I came out saying something like that people would be telling me to stop trying to act black . . .

"Here, look, best song ever. Put it on, okay, ready." She pushed play.

Hey Jude, don't make it bad
Take a sad song and make it better.
Remember to let her into your heart
Then you can start to make it better

"Roxanne, The Beatles, Beast."
"Yea, I think so."
"I know, they're so flippin' cool."
Every day for the next couple months I walked up and down the streets with Beth and Hayley, singing. We'd go home and play it over and over again. We even learned to play the melody on the piano. It was our song.

But really it was their song, not mine. I couldn't stand it at first. It was slow and boring. If it had like a really hot beat behind it, maybe I could have listened and even liked it. They should have made a reggeaton remix, that would have been funny. But instead, every day, the same song ended up on my ipod with one headphone in my ear and one in either Beth's or Hayley's. Once I got close to my block I ended up changing it to "Let's Get Down" by Bow Wow, or anything I could bounce my head to. After a few weeks, "Hey Jude" became my most played tune on Itunes. Its play count was at 96 times. But I didn't care. Beth and Hayley thought it was cool, and they were my friends. I needed them.

Humorous Student Memoirs

A distant cousin, now teaching in Israel, was eager to bring memoir writing into her high school classroom and asked to read an early draft of this book. She found the student excerpts extremely helpful, but noted that most of them were "depressing." Aren't there any examples that are funny? she wanted to know. Many of the boys in her class, and even some of the girls, were starting to get turned off by how heavy the stories were.

Although I did not consciously include only "depressing" examples (and would dispute the choice of word), it is true that most of the best-written memoirs I have received over the years have been quite serious. It is very difficult to write deeply and meaningfully in a comic voice, and few of my eighth graders over the years have even attempted to do so. I confess that I do not push humorous writing, largely because I do not know how to teach somebody to be funny. But I do think there is a place for humor in memoir, and I know firsthand that students really enjoy writing that makes them laugh. As such, I make it a point to read aloud and to recommend humorous published memoirs to the students in my class. These include *First French Kiss* by Adam Bagdasarian (2002), *Kick Me* by Paul Feig (2002), *Bossypants* by Tina Fey (2011), *Running with Scissors* by Augusten Burroughs (2002), and almost everything written by David Sedaris.

Following are excerpts from student memoirs that made me laugh out loud, or at least brought a smile to my face.

FROM *FAMILY CIRCUS*

Welcome to my life. The Circus. Literally. Ever since I can remember my parents have been in the arts . . . My dad's an actor, and he also has another . . . um . . . interesting profession. He's a clown. You read right. MY DAD IS A CLOWN . . . Through my dad being a clown I realized how different my family is. I don't know why, but sometimes I get really ashamed of the fact that my father is a clown. I guess it might have started when people started getting a little weirded out by it . . .

Discussions we have can get weird too. My dad's always trying to get into discussions about life. He tried to give me the sex talk this year! How messed up is that? . . .

"Rosa—Boys do not like girls who are sluts."

"What? Where the hell does that come from? I'm like doing homework."

"I don't care what your friends do. You are not going to be a slut. Not on my watch."

"Huh?"

"You are not a sex pot! I don't care what you think! You are the farthest thing from it!"

"Okay . . . Um . . . I'm going to listen to some music now." I grabbed my iPod.

"Don't you tune me out! You will not be a slut!" . . .

Rosa is even funnier in recreating her first encounter with a "JAPPY" girl she meets at camp.

> "Hi. Who the hell are you?"
>
> "Um . . . Rosa."
>
> "Oh, I like your name. I'm Sabrina. People call me Scrunch or Sab, but you can't call me those unless you're a really hot boy or really best friend."
>
> "Oh."
>
> "Well, don't you like my name? I already said I liked yours! I don't even like your name that much and I said it. What's your problem anyway?"
>
> "Um . . . You have a pretty name?" I wasn't sure how to react to her. She was scaring me.
>
> "Was that like a question?" She cracked her watermelon bubbalicious gum . . . "So where you from?"
>
> "Um . . . New York."
>
> "Oh cool! So like, have you ever been robbed?"
>
> "What?"
>
> "Have you ever been robbed?"
>
> "Um . . . no."
>
> "Have you ever been like . . . stabbed?"
>
> I started laughing right then and there . . .

FROM *MIMICKING THE MOCKINGBIRD*

While I was in 4th or 5th grade, my Dad thought it would be a good idea for me to read To Kill a Mockingbird *by Harper Lee. This was a pretty rational idea, considering that* To Kill a Mockingbird *is one of the best American novels of all time, but for the more special reason my name was Harper Lee as well. However, unless I was some history freak (which I wasn't) or a child genius (which I definitely wasn't) my comprehension level of one of the best American novels at age nine was probably very low. But in my Dad's eyes, that was beside the fact and there was no way out of it . . . While my dad started reading . . . out loud to not just me, but the rest of my family, he would try to imitate a southern accent, which was so brutally painful, it almost sounded Jamaican. I would glance at the clock: 7:45. Then Dad would read some pages, I would go to the bathroom a couple of times, and I would glance at the clock again, to make sure we weren't going past*

8:30. *As my eyes turned from the somewhat intricate floor to the flashing green numbers of hell, the clock read 7:47. Now that I realized that I was going to live my entire life and die in that very chair, I did what any kid would do to take their mind off something: distract myself. The story would make me go off with tangents in my mind.* "Scout would then jump off the tire swing," my dad would say. *Scout ... like Girl Scout cookies? Girl Scout cookies are sooo good. I wish I had some thin mints right now ... It wasn't a story in my field of interest. I was way more into Club Penguin at the time than I was with racism in Alabama. It was all "rape and injustice" wow so cool, but really I just sat in the orange chair in my living room ... with thoughts that I would be there for all of eternity. I thought picking my cuticles would be a better way to spend my time, so by the end of the book my fingers were bloody and covered in scabs ...*

This was also my first encounter with the n-word. My dad could have chosen to skip over it or say "the n-word" but instead he said something along the lines of, "Harper, Claire this book says a word you should never ever use, ever. Now, since it's written in the text, I am going to say it so you have the full southern experience." It wasn't as though we were going on a vacation to Montgomery, Alabama in the 1930s, but at least we had the native language. I hate it when my parents swear, so I said, "But Dad, can't you use another word like watermelon or something?"

"Harper, when you read this book to your kids, you may decide to do that. I am going to read this book to you the way I think that you should hear it."

"But-"

"Nope."

"Okay."

He would then proceed to read, only to come to the classic comprehension drill. We would have to discuss what happened in the chapters we just read.

"Harper, why did Jem get a cake, while Scout and Dill only got a slice of cake?"

"Because he ... he liked cake more?"

"No."

"It was because ... because he was an adult and adults get more cake."

"Possibly."

"Was it chocolate cake?"

"Claire, be quiet." ...

Overall, the first time I read To Kill a Mockingbird *consisted of mostly "And then Atticus Finch —Claire, sit down. One . . . Two . . ." and "Dad, can I puh-lease go to the bathroom," but as it is a result of my name, it could not have been avoided. Sometimes I talk to my mom about it, looking back on the past, and each time she tells me that in the future, I'm going to be telling my kids the story of how I sat through my dad's reading of* To Kill a Mockingbird *and how I loved every minute of it. Sometimes I believe her and other times I laugh because of how ridiculous the thought of having more than one kid seems.*

FROM *THE TIME I FOUND MY COUSIN IN A PORN VIDEO*

It was Christmas Eve, and the spirit of atheism was running high in the family. My Muslim cousin Jack was scarfing down bacon next to the fire, my ten year old little cousin was writing a letter to Santa complaining about elf cruelty, and someone had taken a picture of baby Jesus that was hanging on the wall and taped a picture of Steven Colbert over his face. Worst of all, though, was my dad, who was illustrating in no vague terms that he thought religion was stupid.

"See that bacon you're eating, Ellen?" he said, sipping his third glass of wine that night. "The pig that steak came from died to save all the other pigs from sin."

Ellen rolled her eyes, brushing her dark-brown bangs from her face. "James, just because I believe something you don't doesn't mean you have to attack me for it."

"Whoa, I'm not attacking anyone. I'm just saying that bacon came from Pig Jesus." . . .

Ellen had just turned twenty one, but out of all my cousins above twenty, she was easily the most innocent, most responsible one. She'd never make fun of anyone behind their back, never got drunk, never said the word "retarded" on pain of being politically incorrect . . . Even though she was much older than me, there was still kind of a childlike innocence about some parts of her, which is probably why she believed in God . . .

There were just two people missing from the room that day: my uncle, who had been urgently summoned to D.C. on account of some political thing, and my cousin Alan, who had grabbed his dad's computer the second he left and locked himself in his room with it. He had spent the past three days almost entirely in the room, only coming out to eat or go skiing . . . nobody knew for sure what was going on in there. A few brave adults had ventured near the door to ask him what he was doing, to which he would quickly respond, "I'm doing homework really hard right now! If you come in I'll lose my concentration . . .

The first thing that hit me about [Alan's] room was the smell. It smelled really, really weird, and I couldn't quite place what it was. I guess Alan has been working so hard he hasn't showered, *I thought to myself, but it didn't really smell like sweat. The whole scene was remarkably odd . . .*

Alan's face lit up. "C'mere. I'm gonna show you something, but you promise not to tell anyone, okay?"

"Sure, okay," I said. I didn't know something like homework could be so secretive to Alan, but I guess as long as he was doing it, it was all good.

I looked at the screen.

It wasn't homework.

I pushed the screen away from me and scooted across the room to a particularly milk-stained portion of the floor across the room. A number of questions were going through my head, namely: "Dear cousin, why are you showing me a porn video?" or "Dear cousin, why'd you stop working on homework?" or "What were those elephants doing in the top-right corner of the screen?"

Out of shock, though, I instead looked back at his desktop and said dumbly, "What is that?"

It was quite obvious what it was, actually. Alan was on some porn blog and was watching a video from a college party, where two blindfolded girls were making out . . .

I leaned back, flicking one of the masses of Kleenexes around the room off of me. Which was weird, because Alan didn't seem sick at all. "Why exactly should I see this?"

Alan paused the video, pointing to one of the two girls in that blindfolded lip-lock. "Does she look familiar to you?"

"No." What was he expecting me to say? As a fourteen year old, I'm not acquainted with too many porn stars.

Alan grunted. "Look again. Are you sure *it's not anyone you know?"*

"Alan, there's no way I could-" and then I stopped, because the blindfolded girl did look a little familiar. Very familiar, actually. Of course, it was hard to tell with the blindfold on (and, you know, with her face pressed against another girl), and I didn't want to admit it to Alan, but she did look a whole lot like —

"Ellen," Alan said . . .

FROM *A BOY'S LIFE*

"Ewwwww, Mom, this shirt is yucky."

"What are you talking about Nathan you look adorable in it."

"Adorable is for girls, this shirt makes me look like a girl. I don't want to wear it."

"Nathan, you're just as cute as the Energizer Bunny. People will think you look handsome."

Handsome? Ha, yeah, right, humiliating is what I'd call it. A pre-school boy with a pink shirt, a color for girls, would be beaten up and picked on for dressing like a girl. That's exactly what happened to me. My pre-school reputation was in the gutter thanks to my mother's pink hockey shirt . . .

When I got to school all the boys, and even the girls, started picking on me by calling me things like "Girlyman", "Energizer Bunny", Gummy Bear", "Rainbow." . . . When it came to lunch I was left isolated on one half of the table, when it came to recess the boys wouldn't let me play "Duck, Duck, Goose" with them, and when it came to playing with toys and building Lego the boys didn't want me to play with them. I guess the shirt was bad luck and the worst part about it was that it itched like crazy. By the end of the day I felt real sad and I grew an amazing hate for the pink hockey shirt.

Now my mother knew I hated the shirt. I even told her how the other kids hated it too, but she didn't care. She constantly made me wear the shirt, it became her favorite shirt of mine. Every week I was forced to wear it at least once or twice. It grew onto me like fungus, and I hated the shirt. I wanted to burn it or throw it away . . .

On January 30th, my fourth birthday, a miracle happened. Well, I guess everyone gets lucky on his birthday. My mother decided I should celebrate my birthday at school with all of my classmates, and, of course, on that day she dressed me in the pink hockey shirt. A large cake and cranberry juice was brought into the class to share. As the teacher went around the class pouring cranberry juice into cups, an unfortunate accident happened. As my friend Todd leaned over the table to say "Happy Birthday" his elbow hit my cup filled with cranberry juice. I watched carefully as the dark red cranberry juice splashed over the table, making its way onto me, onto the pink hockey shirt. My teacher made me take off the wet and stained pink shirt and finally I felt like a boy again. The other boys thought so too. They treated me with respect, let me play with them in their little games; never was I so glad to take off the pink hockey shirt.

When I showed the cranberry juice stain on my shirt to my mother, she became so frustrated. It was like a piece of her had died. But it wasn't the end of the pink hockey shirt; my mother brought it to the dry cleaners. There they took off the stain but the greatest part was that they accidentally shrunk it about two sizes, leaving it too small for me. So the pink hockey shirt ended up going to my sister, the way it should have from the start.

FROM *SAME OLD JETS*

Being born in a family of Jets fans is akin to being born with a chronic and degenerative genetic disease. The symptoms? A lifetime of false hope, extreme pessimism, betrayals, and letdowns. From the minute I was born, I was sentenced to a lifetime of this. My dad always tells me that his only flaw as a father was raising me to follow in his footsteps as a devoted Jets fan. It's not just that the Jets are consistently a hopelessly mediocre team (which they are). They just always are finding new ways to screw up.

The Jets' finest moment came 44 years ago, when they upset the Baltimore Colts in Super Bowl 3 following Broadway Joe Namath's guarantee of a win. Since then, it's basically all been downhill. I've actually lived through one of the most successful stretches in Jets history (two AFC championship appearances) but I still know the cursed life of Jets fans all too well. This is exhibited clearly at Jets games and when I watch games on TV with my Dad—in both cases, grumblings of "same old Jets" run rampant. The unfortunate saying has come to define a franchise. While the actual success of the Jets (or lack thereof) makes being a Jets fan torturous, the worst thing about being Jets fans is their unwavering loyalty. I am no different from the hordes of Jets fans who are attached to their teams no matter what—and who live with the consequences.

*   *   *

"Dad, I'm freezing my ass off out here," I mumbled, my teeth chattering uncontrollably. He chuckled, but I wasn't kidding. I was legitimately worried that my ass would freeze off. I shook my leg a few times to try and get the blood flowing through my frost covered limbs, but it was all in vain. Even the hot chocolate I had bought was starting to freeze over. However, after a few minutes, I barely even noticed my frozen ass, frost covered legs or cold hot chocolate—all I could think about was the merciless beat down that my Jets were inflicting on the Bengals . . .

"It's cold as a witch's teat out here!" my dad hollered, just as he always does when the weather dips below 40 degrees. And I, as I always did when he screamed this, looked away and pretended like I didn't know him. Looking back on it, he was more incorrect than immature. There is absolutely no way that anything—a "witch's teat" included, could have been as cold as that night.

"The Jets really look unstoppable tonight," I said to no one in particular, pulling my hat further down on my head to shield myself from the unrelenting wind. Right on cue, the Jets ran for no gain.

"Same old Jets," the large black man lamented, between his sips of beer, and sloppy cramming of peanuts into his mouth. He seemed to be holding up just fine in the cold weather, while I needed to be thawed in a microwave to make it out of the game alive. At that moment, I wanted nothing more than to be a large, warm black man, sipping beer and cramming peanuts into my mouth sloppily—but I was stuck in the body of a scrawny, nine year old Jewish kid.

< 160 >

Appendix C: Bibliography of Recommended Memoirs for Middle and High School Students

I have tried to group titles by age appropriateness, but teachers should use their own judgment and knowledge of their students to determine which books are best for their classes.

Grades 6 and Up

Bagdasarian, Adam. 2002. *First French Kiss and Other Traumas.* New York: Farrar, Straus and Giroux.

Cleary, Beverly. 1998. *A Girl from Yamhill.* New York: Dell.

Dahl, Roald. 1986. *Boy.* New York: Puffin.

———. 1988. *Going Solo.* New York: Puffin.

Jiang, Ji Li. 1997. *Red Scarf Girl: A Memoir of the Cultural Revolution.* New York: Scholastic.

Lobel, Anita. 1998. *No Pretty Pictures: A Child of War.* New York: Avon.

Myers, Walter Dean. 2001. *Bad Boy: A Memoir.* New York: HarperTempest.

Satrapi, Marjane. 2003. *Persepolis: The Story of a Childhood.* New York: Pantheon.

———. 2004. *Persepolis 2: The Story of a Return.* New York: Pantheon.

Small, David. 2009. *Stitches: A Memoir.* New York: W.W. Norton.

Spinelli, Jerry. 1998. *Knots in My Yo-Yo String: The Autobiography of a Kid.* New York: Knopf.

Grades 8 and Up

Angelou, Maya. 1997. *I Know Why the Caged Bird Sings.* New York: Bantam.

Beah, Ishmael. 2007. *A Long Way Gone: Memoirs of a Boy Soldier.* New York: Farrar, Straus and Giroux.

< 161 >

Beals, Melba Pattillo. 1994. *Warriors Don't Cry: A Searing Memoir of the Battle to Integrate Little Rock's Central High*. New York: Pocket Books.

Canada, Geoffrey. 1995. *Fist Stick Knife Gun: A Personal History of Violence*. New York: Beacon.

Crutcher, Chris. 2003. *King of the Mild Frontier: An Ill-Advised Autobiography*. New York: Greenwillow.

Dumas, Firoozeh. 2003. *Funny in Farsi: A Memoir of Growing Up Iranian in America*. New York: Villard.

Feig, Paul. 2002. *Kick Me: Adventures in Adolescence*. New York: Three Rivers.

Fey, Tina. 2011. *Bossypants*. New York: Little, Brown.

Fisher, Antwone Quenton. 2001. *Finding Fish: A Memoir*. New York: Harper.

Gantos, Jack. 2002. *Hole in My Life*. New York: Farrar, Straus and Giroux.

Hickam, Homer H., Jr. 2000. *Rocket Boys*. New York: Delta.

Kamkwamba, William, and Bryan Mealer. 2009. *The Boy Who Harnessed the Wind: Creating Currents of Electricity and Hope*. New York: William Morrow.

Kaysen, Susanna. 1994. *Girl, Interrupted*. New York: Vintage.

Lerner, Betsy. 2003. *Food and Loathing: A Life Measured Out in Calories*. New York: Simon and Schuster.

McBride, James. 1996. *The Color of Water: A Black Man's Tribute to His White Mother*. New York: Riverhead Books.

Merrell, Billy. 2003. *Talking in the Dark*. New York: Push.

Oppenheimer, Mark. 2010. *Wisenheimer: A Childhood Subject to Debate*. New York: Free Press.

Runyon, Brent. 2004. *The Burn Journals*. New York: Knopf.

Santiago, Esmeralda. 1993. *When I Was Puerto Rican*. New York: Vintage.

Schutz, Samantha. 2006. *I Don't Want to Be Crazy*. New York: Scholastic.

Thurber, James. 1999. *My Life and Hard Times*. New York: Harper Perennial Modern Classics.

Vizzini, Ned. 2000. *Teen Angst? Naaah*. New York: Random House.

Walls, Jeannette. 2005. *The Glass Castle*. New York: Scribner.

Welty, Eudora. 1984. *One Writer's Beginnings*. Cambridge, MA: Harvard University Press

Wiesel, Elie. 1982. *Night.* New York: Bantam.

Wolff, Tobias. 1989. *This Boy's Life.* New York: The Atlantic Monthly Press.

———. 1994. *In Pharaoh's Army: Memories of the Lost War.* New York: Knopf.

Grades 10 and Up

Baker, Russell. 1982. *Growing Up.* New York: Plume Books.

Burroughs, Augusten. 2002. *Running with Scissors.* New York: Picador.

———. 2004. *Dry.* New York: Picador.

Carroll, Jim. 1987. *The Basketball Diaries.* New York: Penguin.

Conroy, Frank. 1977. *Stop-Time.* New York: Penguin.

Flynn, Nick. 2004. *Another Bullshit Night in Suck City.* New York: W.W. Norton.

Gilman, Susan Jane. 2005. *Hypocrite in a Pouffy White Dress: Tales of Growing Up Groovy and Clueless.* New York: Grand Central.

Hong Kingston, Maxine. 1975. *The Woman Warrior.* New York: Vintage International.

Karr, Mary. 1998. *The Liar's Club: A Memoir.* New York: Penguin.

Obama, Barack. 2004. *Dreams from My Father.* New York: Three Rivers.

Shteyngart, Gary. 2014. *Little Failure.* New York: Random House.

Smith, Patti. 2010. *Just Kids.* New York: HarperCollins.

References

Ambrose, Stephen. 2003. *To America: Personal Reflections of an Historian*. New York: Simon & Schuster.

Angelou, Maya. 1997. *I Know Why the Caged Bird Sings*. New York: Bantam.

Auster, Paul. 1982. *The Invention of Solitude*. New York: Penguin.

Bagdasarian, Adam. 2002. *First French Kiss and Other Traumas*. New York: Farrar, Straus and Giroux.

Baker, Russell. 1987. "Life with Mother." In *Inventing the Truth: The Art and Craft of Memoir*, ed. William Zinsser. Boston: Houghton Mifflin.

Beah, Ishmael. 2007. *A Long Way Gone: Memoirs of a Boy Soldier*. New York: Farrar, Straus and Giroux.

Beals, Melba Pattillo. 1994. *Warriors Don't Cry: A Searing Memoir of the Battle to Integrate Little Rock's Central High*. New York: Pocket Books.

Bomer, Katherine. 2005. *Writing a Life: Teaching Memoir to Sharpen Insight, Shape Meaning—and Triumph Over Tests*. Portsmouth, NH: Heinemann.

Burroughs, Augusten. 2002. *Running with Scissors*. New York: Picador.

Calkins, Lucy McCormick. 1994. *The Art of Teaching Writing*. 2nd ed. Portsmouth, NH: Heinemann.

Dillard, Annie. 1987. "To Fashion a Text." In *Inventing the Truth: The Art and Craft of Memoir*, ed. William Zinsser. Boston: Houghton Mifflin.

Elliott, Stephen. 2009. *The Adderall Diaries*. Saint Paul: Graywolf.

Feig, Paul. 2002. *Kick Me: Adventures in Adolescence*. New York: Three Rivers.

Fey, Tina. 2011. *Bossypants*. New York: Little, Brown.

Fitzgerald, F. Scott. 1995. *F. Scott Fitzgerald: A Life in Letters*. New York: Scribner.

Fletcher, Ralph. 1992. *What a Writer Needs*. Portsmouth, NH: Heinemann.

Flynn, Nick. 2004. *Another Bullshit Night in Suck City*. New York: W.W. Norton.

Frey, James. 2003. *A Million Little Pieces*. New Brunswick: Doubleday.

———. 2006. Interview by Larry King, *Larry King Live*, CNN, January 11. http://www.cnn.com/TRANSCRIPTS/0601/11/lkl.01.html.

Frost, Robert. 1916. "The Road Not Taken." In *Mountain Interval*. New York: Henry Holt and Company.

Gallagher, Kelly. 2011. *Write Like This*. Portland, ME: Stenhouse.

Garrett, George. 1960. "The Last of the Spanish Blood." *Virginia Quarterly Review*, Spring.

Hitchcock, Alfred (director). 1963. *The Birds* (film). Universal Studios.

Kaysen, Susanna. 1994. *Girl, Interrupted*. New York: Vintage.

Kinsella, W.P. 1982. *Shoeless Joe*. Boston: Houghton Mifflin.

Kirby, Dawn Latta, and Dan Kirby. 2007. *New Directions in Teaching Memoir: A Studio Workshop Approach*. Portsmouth, NH: Heinemann.

Lee, Harper. 1960. *To Kill a Mockingbird*. Philadelphia: J.B. Lippincott.

Melville, Herman. 1851. *Moby-Dick*. New York: Harper & Brothers.

Merrell, Billy. 2003. *Talking in the Dark*. New York: Push.

National Governors Association Center for Best Practices, Council of Chief State School Officers (NGA/CCSSO). 2010a. *English Language Arts Standards: Writing: Grade 8*. http://www.corestandards.org/ELA-Literacy/W/8.

National Governors Association Center for Best Practices, Council of Chief State School Officers (NGA/CCSSO). 2010b. *Common Core State Standards for English Language Arts & Literacy in History/Social Studies, Science, and Technical Subjects: Appendix A: Research Supporting Key Elements of the Standards*. http://www.corestandards.org/assets/Appendix_A.pdf.

Rukeyser, Muriel. 2013. *Elegies*. New York: New Directions.

Runyon, Brent. 2004. *The Burn Journals*. New York: Knopf.

Salinger, J. D. 1951. *The Catcher in the Rye*. New York: Little, Brown.

Satrapi, Marjane. 2003. *Persepolis: The Story of a Childhood*. New York: Pantheon.

Shakespeare, William. 1603. *Hamlet*. London: Nicholas Ling and John Trundell.

Small, David. 2009. *Stitches*. New York: W.W. Norton.

The Smoking Gun. 2006. "A Million Little Lies: Exposing James Frey's Fiction Addiction." *The Smoking Gun*. http://www.thesmokinggun.com/documents/celebrity/million-little-lies.

Spielberg, Steven. 1987. Academy Awards Acceptance Speech. Presented March 30.

Tomlinson, Carol Ann, and Susan Demirsky Allan. 2000. *Leadership for Differentiating Schools & Classrooms.* Alexandria, VA: Association for Supervision & Curriculum Development.

Twain, Mark. 1885. *The Adventures of Huckleberry Finn.* New York: Charles L. Webster.

Walls, Jeannette. 2005. *The Glass Castle.* New York: Scribner.

Wizner, Jake. 2007. *Spanking Shakespeare.* New York: Random House.

Wolff, Tobias. 1989. *This Boy's Life.* New York: The Atlantic Monthly Press.

———. 2001. "War and Memory." The New York Times, April 28.

Zinsser, William, ed. 1987. *Inventing the Truth: The Art and Craft of Memoir.* Boston: Houghton Mifflin.

———. 2006. "How to Write a Memoir." *The American Scholar,* March 1. https://theamericanscholar.org/how-to-write-a-memoir/#.VSVxN_nF_tI.

< 166 >

Index